Gentle, loving guidance for emerging victoriously from life's battles.

Here in one volume are the three books from Corrie ten Boom's "Jesus Is Victor" Series: **He Cares, He Comforts, He Sets the Captive Free,** and **Don't Wrestle, Just Nestle.** Drawing from her lifelong walk with the Lord, she reveals how God can work a glorious transformation in every area of life.

In **He Cares, He Comforts,** Corrie deals with the difficult subjects of pain, death, deformity, shame, and abandonment. She recounts her experiences with the sick and dying people she met in the course of her travels. She describes how God gave each of them comfort and assurance which allowed them to rejoice in the midst of their afflic- tion. She urges you to look to Jesus for spiritual healing in times of physical suffering.

In **He Sets the Captive Free,** Corrie delivers a powerful message on the freedom and forgiveness found in God's love. She shares with you the faith that sustained her in prisons and concentration camps, where she learned to acquire the spirit of forgiveness. By trusting God, you can find release from physical or spiritual bondage.

In **Don't Wrestle, Just Nestle,** Corrie shows us how to relieve the pressures of twentieth-century living. She reminds us that if we trust Him, Christ will lift the burden of fear and anxiety. In her warm and touching style, she encourages us to remain in obedience to God to find true peace and security.

With **Jesus Is Victor,** you'll find hope, joy, and personal fulfillment in following Corrie's call to rely on Christ.

Jesus is Victor

Corrie ten Boom

Fleming H. Revell
A Division of Baker Book House Co
Grand Rapids, Michigan 49516

Library of Congress Cataloging-in-Publication Data

Ten Boom, Corrie.
    Jesus is victor.

    "Power books."
    Contents: He cares, He comforts—He sets the captive free—Don't wrestle, just nestle.
    1. Christian life—1960-   2. Ten Boom, Corrie.
3. World War, 1935-1945—Personal narratives, Dutch.
4. Ravensbrück (Germany : Concentration camp)
5. Consolation.   I.   Title.
BV 4501.2.T382   1985   841337
ISBN: 0-8007-5176-0

Tenth printing, October 1993

Printed in the United States of America

Contents

Part One   He Cares, He Comforts

	Preface	13
	Dear Friend	15
	"Jesus Heard You . . . ."	17
1	That Wee Little Baby	18
2	The Little Lamb	20
3	A Happy Visit	22
4	Pain	24
5	Can You Forgive?	26
6	The Foolishness of God	29
7	Alice	31
8	Tommy	33
9	Toontje	35
10	Mother	37
11	Pietje	40
12	Debbie	42
13	Passing the Baton	46
14	Used by God	48
15	Nobody Is Too Bad	50

16 Niwanda   52
17 His Sheep   54
18 Little Angel   56
19 The Lost Sheep   57
20 Worry   59
21 Our Times Are in God's Hands   62
22 When I Saw Death   64
23 Are You Afraid to Die?   66

    "Are You Going Home?"   68
    You Have His Word   69

Part Two   He Sets the Captive Free

    Preface   73
1   I Was in Prison   75
2   Why I Was Sent to Prison   78
3   Solitary Confinement   79
4   The Interrogation   81
5   Ravensbruck   85
6   Does He Forget Me?   87
7   The Lifeline   89
8   A Storm Laid Down   90
9   No Wilderness, the Lord's Garden   92
10 Is Forgiveness Possible?   94
11 Lizzy   96
12 The Red Ticket   98
13 Ask More—He Will Give   100
14 Is a *No* Answer an Answer?   102
15 Freedom   104
16 Kimio   107
17 Joy? Is That Possible?   109

18   Three Decent Sinners   112
19   Hi, Brother!   114
20   Corrie's Message   117
21   Conversations in Prisons   119
        Ann
        Frank
        Roger
22   Mike   123
23   Joe   126
24   So Long!   128
        Appendix of Helpful Sciptures   130

Part Three   Don't Wrestle, Just Nestle

     Foreword   137
 1   Prescription for Anxiety   139
 2   No Time for Anxiety   148
 3   Worry   155
 4   May a Christian Worry?   162
 5   Fear   169
 6   Frustration   179
 7   Don't Burden Yourself   185
 8   Prayer   191
 9   God's Answers to Prayer   197
10   Trust   203
11   Surrender   212

JESUS IS VICTOR

Part One

He Cares, He Comforts

Preface

Through my traveling over the world, and through my books and films, I have made many friends. When they are ill, I should love to be able to visit and comfort each of them. But I do pray for them, and the Lord gave me this idea—to write them a letter!

That was the beginning of this book. I prayed that the Lord would guide me and give me the thoughts, remembering what I had experienced with sick friends, and He gave me one after the other.

Often friends have the same problem, the same kind of suffering, and that's why I wrote down all I could remember. I'm sure that when a friend is sick he or she will find in one of these stories an answer that the Lord has given me when I needed it.

It is the Lord who has helped me to remember. So I hope that my friends will read this book as a message that the Lord gave—to me, for them.

Dear Friend

You are one of the many people who know me, perhaps even one of the many I have met on my recent journeys, an acquaintance who read one of my books, heard me talk, or saw me on film. And so there grew a real fellowship between you and me. I asked the Lord to give me an opportunity to meet you and He gave me this privilege of writing. He caused me to remember visits, experiences that I had with other sick people, and I'm sure that in these you will find an answer to the question *Why?* or to another problem that you have to face.

My friends had to endure suffering and now you are in the same kind of trouble. I prayed to the Lord to give me a word of comfort and an answer and I wrote them down. I think one of these stories that I tell may be an answer for you, from Corrie, but given to Corrie by the Lord Himself. Oh, it was wonderful that the Lord gave me the thoughts and the answers so quickly! So in some way it is a greeting, a message from the Lord Himself, who loves you and has your life in His hands, who knows of every suffering, every problem, as no human being does.

If you do not know Him, this book will be a challenge, an invitation from the Lord, who said:

Come unto me, all that ... are heavy laden, and I will give
you rest.

Matthew 11:28

And if you know Him already, it will be a message from that
Friend you and I have in Jesus.

Perhaps you are too ill, too weak to talk much with Him,
but then you may lay your weak hand in the strong hand of
Him who said:

... him that cometh to me I will in no wise cast out.

John 6:37

How He loves you!

"Jesus Heard You . . . ."

Jesus heard when you prayed last night.
He talked with God about you.
Jesus was there when you fought your fight,
He is going to bring you through.

Jesus knew when you shed those tears,
you did not weep alone.
The burdens you thought too heavy to bear,
He made them His very own.

Jesus Himself was touched by that trial,
you could not understand.
Jesus stood by as you almost fell
and lovingly clasped your hand.

Jesus cared when you bore that pain,
indeed, He bore it too.
He felt each pain, each ache in your heart,
because of His love for you.

Jesus, your Saviour, will always be with you,
no need to be anxious or fret.
Wonderful love, He will be there all the time,
He has never forsaken you yet.

1

That Wee Little Baby

Yesterday I met a lady who is expecting a baby. I always like to pray with such a mother and to pray for the baby she has under her heart.

"Lord Jesus, You love that baby already. You know it and You can already fill that tiny little heart with Your love. Lord, will You give the baby and the mother strength and health for the time of pregnancy? And also for the birth? Bless the doctors and the nurses and give them wisdom and love." I was happy that I could pray with that mother, for I know that the Lord hears our prayers.

Some time after that, I was lying in the sunshine and I think I had fallen asleep, for I had a dream. I was talking with that wee baby for whom I had prayed! Often in dreams things happen that cannot take place in reality, for that little baby was talking with me, too!

"I am very happy to be here in this very safe corner of the world. It is so warm and so quiet here under Mama's heart. I have enough food and I do not at all long to be born! I am sure life must be difficult and noisy! No, I want to stay here always."

In my dream, I answered, "No, you must not think about being born as something that is sad or wrong. It is a joy to be born, for then life, the *real* life, begins. You will see your mother's face and her eyes full of love for you. You will rest in her arms; and, you will feel her arms around you. Then you will grow up and become a strong person. After you have lived for a time, there will come a moment when you have to go through another birth: when you go from this world to heaven. It will be like the time when you came from the little place under your mother's heart into life. Then you will see the eyes of Jesus and you will rest in His arms and He will bring you to a beautiful house that He has been preparing for all who believe in Him."

I awoke, and I had to laugh. But I was also happy about that dream. It was good. I took the Living Bible and read:

> You made all the delicate, inner parts of my body, and knit them together in my mother's womb . . . . You saw me before I was born . . . .
>
> Psalms 139:13, 16 LB

Are you afraid to die? Remember that for a child of God, death is only a passing through to a wonderful new world—to the house with many mansions where Jesus has prepared a place for you.

> For we know that when this tent we live in now is taken down—when we die and leave these bodies—we will have wonderful new bodies in heaven, homes that will be ours forevermore, made for us by God himself, and not by human hands.
>
> 2 Corinthians 5:1 LB

If you don't have that assurance, please read on. I will tell you more about how to be ready.

2

The Little Lamb

It is always a tragic thing when a child dies. People have a tendency to call this an injustice on the part of God. However, God owes us nothing. If He gives our child ten years and then takes him away, we must be grateful for those ten years.

Also, I know how the Lord can use such happenings to accomplish a good purpose. I once heard about a mother who lost her child. She was very embittered and rebellious. One day she walked alone in the fields with a heavy heart. Suddenly she noticed a flock of sheep. The shepherd tried to have the sheep cross over a narrow bridge into another field, but the sheep did not want to set their feet on the shaky little bridge. They went right and left and turned just like stupid sheep do, but they did not obey the shepherd. Finally, the shepherd grabbed a little lamb that had been pressing itself against the soft wool of its mother's body. The man now carried the little lamb across the narrow bridge and put it into the meadow on the other side. Immediately, the mother sheep, bleating loudly, followed across the bridge, and then all the others followed.

The bereaved mother had observed all this with interest. Suddenly she knew that this was a message for her. She realized that for many years she had stubbornly gone her own way instead of following the call of the Good Shepherd: "Come unto me!" Now He had taken away her little son and brought him safely to the other side. His purpose was that she would come to Him, and lead the way for many others to be saved. This is what happened. She went to the Lord and gave Him her heart and life. Then she was able to be a witness to many others and help them to find the way to the Good Shepherd.

3

A Happy Visit

She was the mother of one of my club girls and had asked me to visit her in the hospital. When I arrived, she was lying in a bed in a big ward, and she was looking very happy.

"I am really having the time of my life," she said. "Never have I had such good care. I do not have to cook—they bring my meals to my bed—and the nurses even wash me. My, that is different—quite different—from being at home and taking care of my naughty boys."

I understood what she meant. She lived in a narrow alley and had a rather rough husband and many children. "Oh," she said, "it is such a joy that the nurses look after me in every way! I like being ill."

"I understand, but tell me, are you in pain?"

"Yes," she said, "I still have pain, but I must tell you more about why I am so happy. The woman next to me told me more about Jesus. My daughter, who is in your club, also told me about Him, but here I really had time to think. She gave me a tract and a small Bible. I have been reading them and feel so happy! She read Psalm Twenty-three to me and I understood that the Lord *is* my Good Shepherd. Isn't that wonderful? There is only one almost insurmountable obstacle, and that is that next week I must go home again. I feel happy, but I also feel rather weak. I lost so much blood and I do not feel strong. Then to have to go back and start everyday life again . . . ."

I understood and said to her, "Listen. You know now that the Lord is your Shepherd and takes care of His sheep. When you are at home, the same Jesus, who now gives you peace in your heart, will be your Guide and your Friend. What a Friend we have in Jesus! He will help you with all the work you have to do at home. He helped you here! When I was a little girl, five years old, I asked Jesus to come into my heart, and He became my best Friend. Now that was a long time ago, but I know He never lets you down. At home, you will find that He is your teammate. Do you have difficulties and problems?"

"Yes, I have many. Big boys are not easy these days . . . ."

I could tell her that every person in the world is very important in God's eyes and that Jesus, when He died on the cross, bore our sins and sorrows and our punishment. If she would go to Him, He would in no wise cast her out. I prayed with her, and then I heard her whisper, "Jesus, I did not know You, but I would like to be the sheep that You find and take into Your arms. Will You also forgive me my sins? Amen."

I was happy about that and again I saw that there is nobody in the world who can say, "I cannot come to Jesus, He will not accept me."

Come unto me, all . . . .
Matthew 11:28

He loves you and is very happy if you say, "Yes, Jesus, I want to belong to You."

For God so loved the world, that he gave his only begotten Son, that whosoever believeth in him should not perish, but have everlasting life.
John 3:16

4

Pain

I visited Bob, a friend who had had a terrible accident. When I entered his room, he opened his eyes and looked at me, saying only one word: "Pain." I saw on his face that his suffering was almost unbearable. I stayed with him that evening.

There came a moment when I saw that he was able to listen and I told him an experience I had in the concentration camp. "Bob, the greatest suffering I had in the concentration camp was to be stripped of all my clothing and to have to stand naked. I told my sister, 'I cannot bear this. This is worse than all other cruelties we have had to endure.' Suddenly it was as if I saw Jesus on the cross, and I remembered that it says in the Bible, 'They took His garments.' Jesus hung there naked. By my own suffering, I understood a fraction of Jesus' suffering. And that gave me strength. Now I could bear my own suffering. Love so amazing—so divine—demands my life, my soul, my all. Bob, do you realize it must have meant almost intolerable pain to Jesus to die on the cross? Just think of His hands, His feet, His body. And He did that for you and for me."

I was silent. Bob had closed his eyes. But a moment later he looked at me and said, "I am looking at Jesus. Yes, I understand only a fraction of the pain He suffered. And it makes me so thankful that He did it all for me."

Bob's face was more relaxed than before and I saw peace in his eyes. A moment later I saw that he had fallen asleep and I quietly left the room.

The next day I was able to visit him again. "Corrie," he said, "every time I had so much pain, and could hardly bear it, I was thinking of Jesus. It made me so thankful! It is as if now I have the strength to bear it. Tell me a little bit of what you thought when you had to suffer in the concentration camp. Have you ever had pain?"

"I surely have, and do you know what helped me then?

> The sufferings of this present time are not worthy to be compared with the glory which shall be revealed in us.
> Romans 8:18

"We can look forward to the time when we shall be in the place where there is no pain, no cruelty, no death. Oh, Bob, the best is yet to be! Isn't that a joy?"

I saw him smiling for the first time. "Yes," he said, "what a joy! The best is yet to be!"

> And God shall wipe away all tears from their eyes; and there shall be no more death, neither sorrow, nor crying, neither shall there be any more pain: for the former things are passed away.
> Revelation 21:4

5

Can You Forgive?

One day I visited an old friend in a hospital. When I entered her room, I saw that she was very ill, but also that there was an expression of bitterness on her face. We had many things to talk about, for we had not seen each other for a long time. Then she told me about her husband.

"I know that I will be ill for a long time. The doctor does not give me any hope that I can do my work for a long time to come. My husband did not like having a sick wife. He left me and now lives with a younger woman. He never comes to see me."

"Have you forgiven him?"

"No, I certainly have not!"

"I will tell you something of my own experiences, when I felt bitter about someone. It was in Germany. One day I saw a lady in a meeting who did not look into my eyes. Suddenly I recognized her. She was a nurse who had been very cruel to my dying sister when we were in Ravensbruck Concentration Camp during the war. When I saw her, a feeling of bitterness, almost hatred, came into my heart. How my dying sister had suffered because of her! The moment I felt that hatred in my heart, I knew that I myself had no forgiveness. It was the Lord Jesus who said to us:

If ye forgive not men their trespasses, neither will your Father forgive your trespasses.

Matthew 6:15

"I knew I had to forgive her, but I could not. Then I had a good talk with the Lord about it when I was at home later. 'Lord, you know I cannot forgive her. My sister suffered too much because of her cruelties. I know, Lord, that I must forgive, but I cannot.' Then the Lord gave me:

The love of God is shed abroad in our hearts by the Holy Spirit which is given unto us.

Romans 5:5

"The Lord taught me a prayer: 'Thank You, Lord, for Romans 5:5. Thank You, Jesus, that You brought into my heart God's love by the Holy Spirit who is given to me. Thank You, Father, that Your love in me is stronger than my hatred and bitterness.' The same moment I knew I could forgive.

"I told a friend about my experience and she said, 'Oh, I know that nurse. She works in a hospital not far from here.'

" 'Can you call her?'

" 'Sure I can.' She called the nurse and I had a talk with her over the telephone, telling her that when I had the next meeting that evening, I would have a different message and would very much like her to come.

"Her answer was, 'You would like to see *me* in your meeting?'

" 'Yes, that is why I phoned. I should like it very much.'

" 'Then I will come.' She did come, and during the entire evening she looked into my eyes while I spoke. After the meeting, I had a talk with her. I told her that I had been bitter, but that God's Holy Spirit in me had brought His love instead of hatred and that now I loved her. I told her that it was through Jesus Christ who bore our sins on the cross. He forgave us, but He also fills our hearts with God's love through the Holy Spirit, and that is why I could invite her to come to the second meeting.

"I told her more and at the end of our talk that nurse accepted the Lord Jesus Christ as her personal Saviour and Lord. Do you see the miracle? I, who had hated her, was used by God to bring her to the acceptance of Jesus Christ. Not only will the Lord cleanse us by His blood but He will also use us. He used me, who hated her, and God had so absolutely forgiven and cleansed *me* that He could use me to show *her* the way of salvation!

"You are bitter about your husband, but claim Romans 5:5. I know that you love the Lord Jesus. You have known Him for a long time. Trust Him to do the miracle of bringing into your heart so much of God's love that you can forgive your husband!" I prayed with her and left.

A week later I was once more in her room. When I saw her, I knew that God had done something in her heart. "I am absolutely free. The Lord has done in me such a tremendous miracle that I could forgive my husband. You know, now there is a great peace and joy in me."

Yes, we never touch the ocean of God's love so much as when we love our enemies. It is a joy to *accept* forgiveness, but it is almost a greater joy to *give* forgiveness.

> The love of God is shed abroad in our hearts by the Holy Spirit which is given unto us.
>
> Romans 5.5

6

The Foolishness of God

After World War II, my friends and I organized a former concentration camp in Germany as a shelter for the homeless. Once, when I went there, I found a man (a lawyer) who was seriously ill. I asked him if he knew the Lord Jesus. "No," he said, "as long as I do not understand things with my brains, I cannot believe them."

I had a talk with him and I told him that in the Book of 1 Corinthians, chapters one and two tell us about the wisdom of the wise and the foolishness of God. "In the Bible," I said, "you can read very much about the foolishness of God. It is the highest wisdom. It is more important than the wisdom of the wise, because it is only through this that you get the real vision."

It was some weeks later that once more I was in our camp and I went straight to my friend. He was even more ill than the first time I had seen him. I asked, "What do you think of the foolishness of God?"

"I can praise the Lord, for I have seen that it is the greatest wisdom. I have thrown away my pride and I have come to Jesus as a sinner and asked forgiveness. I thank Him for His death on the cross, and I can tell you that He has brought into my heart a peace that passes all understanding. It surpasses

everything of the wisdom of the wise, but it is the greatest reality I have ever experienced in my life. I am so thankful for
the Bible. During these weeks I have read much in it and I do
not fear the future, whatever happens."

> Neither death, nor life, nor angels, nor principalities, nor
> powers, nor things present, nor things to come, Nor height, nor
> depth, nor any other creature, shall be able to separate us from
> the love of God, which is in Christ Jesus our Lord.
>
> Romans 8:38, 39

For the first time I saw him look really happy!

> ... hath not God made foolish the wisdom of this world? ...
> Because the foolishness of God is wiser than men; and the weak-
> ness of God is stronger than men.
>
> 1 Corinthians 1:20, 25

7

Alice

In the concentration camp, a girl once came to me and said, "Please, will you come to Alice a moment? She has such terrible nights. While we sleep, she always turns from one side to the other. She suffers. I don't know what it is. Can you help her?"

"Sure," I said, "I can help her. I can pray for her. But I am busy here with a group. We are studying a portion of the Bible. In a quarter of an hour I will come to Alice."

When I went to her, I saw that she had fallen asleep. She was very restless, tossing from one side to the other. I spoke softly to her, but she did not hear me. Then I prayed and said, "Lord Jesus, You can fill Alice's heart with Your peace. You can fill her subconscious with Your love and then she will sleep well."

As I said amen to that prayer, I saw that Alice was quiet. She slept and I knew that the Lord had answered my prayer.

The next morning, my friend who had called me the day before said, "Oh, Corrie, it was a joy that Alice slept so well. She was so quiet—and I know that God has answered your prayer."

That day Alice died, but I had enjoyed an experience that has given me much courage. When we pray, every word we

say is heard by the Lord, and I even read in the Book of Revelation that our prayers are kept in heaven. Our intercession is
so important!

Often we cannot reach the others, but the Lord can reach
everyone. What a joy to have such a Saviour!

... pray one for another ....

James 5:16

8

Tommy

He was one of a big family. I believe there were fourteen children. Tommy was at a special school for mentally handicapped persons. I gave Bible lessons in that school.

Sometimes I visited Tommy in his home. When I asked where he was his mother always said, "He's in his room upstairs." I knew where to find him—in the little corner of the attic that was his "room." It was nothing more than a bed and a chair. On the chair there was always a small picture of Jesus on the cross.

I remember that once when I visited him, Tommy was on his knees before that chair. His face was full of joy. "Tommy, why are you so happy?" I asked.

"Because Jesus loves me!" he said. "And I love Jesus. He died on the cross for me and my sins, and now I have forgiveness."

His mother told me that Tommy always went straight to his little room when he came home. It was quiet there—a corner of peace in the rather small house. With so many children, the house was often noisy.

One day she found him with his head on the chair. In his hand was the picture of Jesus. Tommy did not move. He was with the Lord.

I'm sure that when he died, he must have felt great joy, because Jesus loved him and had died for him on the cross— and he knew it! Do you know it, too? Jesus, who loved Tommy, loves you just as much.

For God so loved the world, that he gave his only begotten Son, that whosoever believeth in him should not perish, but have everlasting life.

John 3:16

9

Toontje

In Haarlem, my hometown, there was a minister who told me of a little boy who was feebleminded. His name was Toontje. He was always sitting in the front pew of the church. The minister said to his wife, "Toontje doesn't understand one word of my sermons. Nevertheless, he is so faithful—he comes every Sunday."

Once the pastor spoke of the ocean of God's love and told how we knew of it through Jesus Christ. When he was talking, he saw on Toontje's face an expression of great joy. Toontje understood when he talked about God's love. I myself worked among the feebleminded and I know from experience that you can never speak too much about the love of God.

The next day the pastor went to Toontje's home. He thought he would see if the boy still knew something of God's love. But when he arrived at Toontje's house, he heard that the boy had died in his sleep. The pastor told me that on Toontje's dead face was an expression of heavenly joy. "I believe," he said, "that Toontje tried to get too much of God's love into his heart, so that his heart just broke for joy."

If you and I would also accept too much of God's love, our hearts could break for joy. But in heaven we shall have such strong hearts that they will contain much, much more of the love of God. Oh, what a joy that will be! Then we shall praise and thank Him for all He was and is and shall be, for us. Hallelujah! What a Saviour!

> We can only see a little of the ocean
>   when we stand at the rocky shore,
> But out there, beyond the eye's horizon,
>   there's more—there's more!
>
> We can only see a little of God's loving,
>   a few rich samples of His mighty store,
> But out there, beyond the eye's horizon,
>   there is more—there is more!
>
> AUTHOR UNKNOWN

We can read in the Bible:

> When I think of the greatness of this great plan, I fall on my knees before the Father from whom all fatherhood, earthly or heavenly, derives its name, and I pray that out of the glorious richness of his resources he will enable you to know the strength of the Spirit's inner reinforcement—that Christ may actually live in your hearts by your faith. And I pray that you, firmly fixed in love yourselves, may be able to grasp with all Christians how wide and deep and long and high is the love of Christ—and to know for yourselves that love so far beyond our comprehension. May you be filled through all your being with God himself! Now to him who by his power within us is able to do infinitely more than we ever dare to ask or imagine—to him be glory in the Church and in Christ Jesus forever and ever. Amen!
>
> Ephesians 3:14–21
> (*See* PHILLIPS.)

10

Mother

I would like to tell you a little bit about my mother. I loved her so very much. The last years of her life, she was very ill and she could not even talk well—only a few words. But she could love and she could receive love. It was before she fell ill that we had a talk about the Lord.

Mother said, "I am not quite sure if everything is all right between the Lord and me. My faith is so little."

I told her words of Jesus, such as, "Come unto me, all . . . ." I said, "Mother, you, too, belong to the *all.*"

Mother looked sad and answered, "Yes, but . . . ." These words so often interfere when the Lord speaks to us, if we listen more to the spirit of doubt than to the Lord.

And now Mother was ill. She had had a stroke and could only say a few words. One day, I brought her a breakfast tray. She folded her hands and then shook her head. I asked, "Mother, can you not even find words when you pray?"

"No." But then she looked at me and I saw that her face was relaxed and happy.

"But it does not matter that you cannot talk to the Lord," I said. "He talks to you, doesn't He?"

"Yes," she said, and her face was beaming with joy.

"Is it all right with you and the Lord?"

"Absolutely!" was her reply.

I tried to find out the reason she was so changed from doubt to trust. "Did we say something, Mother? Or did some-one else who visited you, perhaps the pastor who came to see you yesterday? Or was it a message over the radio that gave you the assurance of salvation?"

Mother smiled and then she pointed upward with her fin-ger.

"Was it the Lord who made it all right?"

"Yes, absolutely, it was the Lord." Six words Mother said, and what a joyful sentence!

My! There I saw that even when we could not reach her, the Lord could always reach her. And He is more concerned about our well-being than we are for each other. When I told Father, he said, "Oh, this is an answer to my prayer!"

"Did you also pray for it? I did, too." We found out that the whole family had been praying that the Lord might give Mother great assurance instead of doubt. How He had an-swered that prayer! What a joy it was!

Later on, Mother grew worse and was very, very ill; then she could not talk at all. It was as if she had no consciousness, but I felt her pulse and then I talked and asked her some questions. Her heartbeat went quicker when I spoke. "Mother, when you are going to die, you have nothing to fear, for you know that Jesus died on the cross for the sins of the whole world, and also for your sins. And, Mother, He is preparing a beautiful house for you in heaven. Then you may go there and we shall see each other again. For the Lord loves us and we all love Him! Just think of it, Mother, in heaven we shall have no pain. There will be no sickness at all, and, Mother, there you will see Jesus. What a joy it will be to look at His wonderful face!"

I knew that although she could not speak at all, she had understood what I had said. But do you understand what made me happiest? To know that when we cannot reach the other one, the Lord can reach His beloved. And it is He who has said:

Lo, I am with you alway, even unto the end of the world.
Matthew 28:20

I know that He was with Mother when she died and went home. He Himself brought her into His wonderful paradise. "Promoted to Glory," the Salvation Army people say.

Thou hast beset me behind and before, and laid thine hand upon me.
Psalms 139:5

11

Pietje

Pietje was a hunchback. She was one of my club girls. We liked each other and had a lot of fun. She could neither walk very far nor very fast and I also had difficulty keeping pace with the other girls of my club. I remember we were on a trip one time through Germany, and we had to cross a rather high mountain. Pietje came to me and said, "Auntie, give me your hand and I will help you." We both had to laugh, for she understood that I needed her help and she needed mine, so we stayed a little behind the rest of my healthy club girls and went arm-in-arm up the mountain.

Yes, Pietje was a dear girl. I remember that in the youth hostel where we stayed that evening, we had a talk about the Judgment Day of God. Pietje said, "I'm afraid to come before the Judgment seat. Have we any advocate who will plead for us?"

"Well, just look in the Bible."

Christ . . . maketh intercession for us.

Romans 8:34

"That is good!" Pietje said. "Who is our judge?"
"Read it yourself."

Who is he that condemneth? It is Christ . . . .

Romans 8:34

"What? Jesus Christ is our Judge *and* our Advocate? Now I am not afraid anymore! He will plead us Not Guilty."

That girl was so happy because she saw what a joy it is that Jesus died for us on the cross and carried our punishment. She knew that one day He will be our Judge and our Advocate. Yes, that was a good talk we had together, there in that youth hostel! I remember there was a lovely view over the mountains and the sun was setting with beautiful colors.

Later, I had to visit Pietje when she was very ill. I found her in the corner of a huge ward in a big hospital. When I saw her, there was nobody with her—no visitors and no nurse—and I talked with her.

"Will you stay with me until I die?" she asked.

"Yes," I said, "I'll do that. Are you sure that you will die soon?"

"Yes," Pietje smiled. "I'm not at all afraid, for, you know, my Judge is the Advocate and my Advocate is the Judge. I am not afraid at all, because it is Jesus Himself who loves me and I love Him."

Say, do *you* sometimes fear when you think of the Judgment Day of God, where we all have to appear whether we believe it or not? Read your Bible! Jesus is *your* Judge and *your* Advocate. Isn't that good? We have nothing to fear— *nothing!*

Who is he that condemneth? It is Christ that died, yea rather, that is risen again, who is even at the right hand of God, who also maketh intercession for us.

Romans 8:34

12

Debbie

A friend of mine told me about her sister Debbie. She was very ill and needed some comfort. "I know," my friend said, "that you cannot go all the way to Missouri to visit her, and she cannot come to you. But what about having a talk over the telephone?" That was a good idea. Isn't it wonderful to live in a world where you can talk with each other over the telephone?

It was a good conversation. She told me her difficulties and her worries. "Corrie," she said, "I'm very ill, and some people think I must die. I am afraid of death. Can you help me?"

"Yes, surely, but listen. We haven't much time to talk over the telephone, so let us just ask each other some questions and give answers. Do you know the Lord Jesus? I don't ask if you know *about* Him, but do you *know* Him?"

"I'm not sure. I have not read much in the Bible. I did not go to church and was really not greatly interested in spiritual things, so I feel that I do not really know Jesus."

"Then first of all you must come to Him, for He is the One who can comfort and help you. He said:

Come unto me, all ye that labour and are heavy laden, and I will give you rest.

Matthew 11:28

... him that cometh to me I will in no wise cast out.

John 6:37

"And when you come to Him He is willing to come so close that He will even come into your heart.

> Behold, I stand at the door, and knock: if any man hear my voice, and open the door, I will come in ....
>
> Revelation 3:20

"Do you understand that *you* must open the door? Then He will come in and you can tell Him everything. He understands far more than I—or any other human being—can. It is true that when you come into contact with the Lord Jesus, you will see your sins, but look at the cross then. You must simply say, 'Lord Jesus, forgive me. I thank You that You died on the cross for my sins.' The Bible says that then He will cast your sins into the depths of the sea, forgiven and forgotten. And I believe that He adds a sign that reads NO FISHING ALLOWED! What about that?"

"I will think about it."

"No, listen! It is all right to think about it, but we have so little time now. Why not do it?"

"Do what?"

"Ask Jesus to come into your heart!"

"Is it so simple?"

"Yes, so simple!"

Then I prayed with her. Oh, it is such a joy that we can always pray with one another over the telephone—the line to the Lord is never busy. He is always ready to listen. "Lord, Debbie would like to ask You to come in, and I thank You, Lord, that You are willing. Will You send away all the doubt, all the 'yes, buts' and the 'if onlies'? I thank You, Lord, that You love Debbie. Hallelujah! Amen!

"Now, Debbie, the way is open. Say, 'Come into my heart, Lord Jesus.' "

And she did. I heard her say, "Lord Jesus, come into my heart. I know that I am not good enough, but, oh, Lord, how I need You! Thank You, Jesus, that You came into my heart. I will tell You all the sins I can remember and I thank You that You have borne them on the cross. Oh, Lord Jesus, You love me, thank You. And I love You. Amen."

Now, wasn't that a wonderful prayer? I was so happy and I know the Lord was happy. I could imagine Him standing there with His arms wide open. I said also, "Debbie, now tell Him all your fears and problems and be sure that when you feel very ill, the Lord Jesus is with you. He will not let you down for one moment."

"Are you sure?"

"Yes, for I know the Lord. I have known Him for a long time and He never gives in. And you two will win, Jesus and you. Bye, Debbie. Until we meet, not in Missouri, but there—in heaven."

"Thank you, Corrie."

I was so happy about that telephone call. But I could do something more for her, and that was to pray! And I did: "Lord, make her very conscious of Your presence. And, Lord, surround her with Your angels and let her room be a room where she is together with You and the angels."

Some time afterward, I met her sister again and she said, "Oh, Corrie, very shortly after you had spoken with Debbie, she became more ill and I went to her to be with her until the end. She repeated all you had said over the telephone. 'I did it,' Debbie told me. 'I didn't understand everything but I know that He came, for since that time there has been such peace and joy and there is no fear at all. I know that I have to die soon, but do you know that I long to go to be with the Lord in heaven?' "

What a blessed telephone talk that was!

Jesus did it,
The Bible tells it,
I believe it.
That settles it!

Come unto me, all ye that labour and are heavy laden, and I will give you rest.

Matthew 11:28

13

Passing the Baton

You know that I am a *Tramp for the Lord.* I traveled all over the world to tell others about the Lord Jesus. I am already old and I do not like to go alone. That is why I always have a younger woman with me. At one time, the Lord gave me Connie to accompany me. For more than seven years, we went together over a large part of the world. But she married, and then the Lord gave me another companion.

There came a time when Connie became very ill, and she knew that she had to die.

Her husband came home one evening and saw that she was crying. He put his arm around her and asked, "Connie, why do you cry?"

She answered, "I traveled much with Tante Corrie and after that I traveled much with you. But now I must go on a journey all alone and you and Tante Corrie will not be with me . . . ."

"Oh, but listen, Connie," said her husband. "I will keep your hand in mine, and in the moment when you really die, I will give your hand into the hand of Jesus. He will keep you through the valley of the shadow of death and bring you to the beautiful heaven where He has prepared a house for you!"

Connie did not cry anymore. What her husband had said was so true! And it all happened that way when Connie went home.

Oh, that loving hand of God! The men who wrote the Psalms knew much when they wrote what the Holy Spirit told them:

> If I take the wings of the morning, and dwell in the uttermost parts of the sea; Even there shall thy hand lead me, and thy right hand shall hold me.
>
> Psalms 139:9, 10

> . . . thou art my strength. Into thine hand I commit my spirit.
>
> Psalms 31:4, 5

Connie had a husband who was with her until the last moment of her life. Many, many people have no husband who is able and has the opportunity to stay with them when they are dying, but the great joy is that everyone can know there is a Saviour in Jesus Christ. "What a Friend we have in Jesus!" His hand keeps us, not only when we go through the valley of the shadow of death but also before that. When we pray, "Take my hand, Lord, and hold me tight," the Lord does it. He has every opportunity and every possibility—and how much love He has for us! He is never too busy with others. He takes time to be with us. He himself said:

> Lo, I am with you alway, even unto the end of the world.
>
> Matthew 28:20

My father used to say to us, when we were children and had to go away from home for a while, "Children, don't forget, when Jesus takes your hand, then He holds you tight. And when Jesus keeps you tight, He guides you through life. And when Jesus guides you through life, one day He brings you safely home."

14

Used by God

Once I slept in a hospital in a concentration camp. Many people were ill and many died. In the night, I heard people calling and I went to them. I was ill myself, but not so seriously that I couldn't do this—I went to everyone who called. I saw much, much suffering and loneliness there.

It was in that concentration camp hospital that I experienced God's use of sick people to help others around them. You can feel so weak in illness and unable to do anything, but witnessing for the Lord Jesus is possible because it is really the Lord who witnesses *in us* and it causes us to relax. When we are channels of living water, then it is the Lord who tells us what to say, and He *never* makes a mistake.

Nobody was with these dying people, but I could tell all of them, "Jesus is here. Just put your hand in His hand." And many of them did. And then I saw peace coming into the hearts of these people. There is a little poem in Holland:

> *Als wij de doodsvallei betreen,*
> *laat ons elke aardse vriend alleen,*
> *maar, Hij, de beste Vriend in nood,*
> *geleid ons over graf en dood.*

When we enter the valley of the shadow of death,
all our earthly friends leave us alone,
but He, the best Friend in need,
accompanies us through the grave and death.

Yes, even for people who are surrounded by friends and relatives, a moment comes when they have to turn to Jesus—the only One who can help them. But what a joy that He is there!

I saw a nurse who looked so worried and tired. Every time she passed my bed, a woman next to me smiled to her, and sometimes she said a kind word.

In the evening the nurse came to her and said, "Do you know that you have helped me? My day was full of disappointments, but your smile has encouraged me."

I learned an important lesson that evening.

15

Nobody Is Too Bad

During the war in Vietnam, I was permitted to visit a hospital. I talked to the men who were wounded. In a ward with about twelve patients, I had an opportunity to speak. I told them about the living Jesus, who is with us, who loved us so much that He died for us, and who now lives for us. He is at the same time at the right hand of the Father, praying for us. I also told them that He said:

> Come unto me, all ye that labour and are heavy laden, and I will give you rest.
>
> Matthew 11:28

I showed them what a joy it was that we could come to Him.

Afterwards, I had a talk with the man sitting next to me. He was not much more than a boy, and seriously wounded. He said to me, "What you told about Jesus is so beautiful, so joyful! But I cannot do what you said and go to Him. I have heard about the Lord, but I have always blasphemed. When there were boys in my class who followed the Lord, I teased them. There has been hatred in my heart—hatred against God—and now I know that I am seriously wounded. But I have been too bad, I cannot go to the Lord. I am ashamed of what I have done, of how I have tried to keep others away from Him. Now don't tell me that I can ask Him to help me. I am a very wicked fellow."

"There is only one kind of person who cannot come to Jesus," I told him. "They are the ones who think and say, 'I'm so good, I don't need forgiveness, I don't need the Saviour.' They are the Pharisees, and you can read in the Bible that Jesus could not and would not help the people who were so proud of themselves and who thought they were so good.

"You are quite different. You think you are too bad. You are not. Jesus bore the sins of the whole world and that is a lot. He has also borne your sins on the cross: sins of hatred, of blasphemy, of whatever you did. You *can* go to Him. Jesus hates sins but loves sinners, and all His promises are really for sinners only. *You* are not good enough; *you* are not able. It is *Jesus* who is able and He is your Saviour. Just talk to Him! Tell Him what you have done and what you have been, and then ask forgiveness. The Bible says that when you bring your sins to Him, He will blot them out like a cloud. Did you see that cloud this morning? It is gone. It will never come again. It has absolutely disappeared forever. So when you bring your sins to Jesus, He will make them disappear—He will destroy them forever and ever."

Suddenly I saw that all the men in the ward were listening. I asked, "Who of you will now come to Jesus as a sinner? When you know you are a sinner, you are forgiven." Many men in that ward responded.

> If we confess our sins, he is faithful and just to forgive us our sins, and to cleanse us from all unrighteousness.
>
> 1 John 1:9

16

Niwanda

I saw a little paper in my hand. I don't know who put it there, but it was a letter: "Please, come to me. I am in the fifth bed at the right. Niwanda."

I was in Africa and had spoken that morning in a boys' boarding school. I asked the missionary if he could help me find out from whom that letter had come. He smiled and said, "Yes, I know. That boy is very ill. We could not yet take him to the hospital. Fifth bed, that is in room three. I can take you there."

We entered the room where we found Niwanda. Immediately I saw that he was really ill. "I needed some help to find you, boy!"

We both laughed and the missionary said, "I will leave you alone with him."

Niwanda and I had a good talk together. "Tell me something of yourself, boy."

"I am very ill. I have been a Christian for a long time and I have served God, but when I look back on my life, I feel so ashamed. I read in the Bible that Paul said, 'I have fought a good fight.' When I look at the past, I know that I, too, have really done my best to fight the good fight. But no, I didn't make a good job of it as Paul did."

"Listen, Niwanda. It is true that Paul wrote, 'I have fought the fight.' We can quite agree because we have such great respect for him. But he did not write, 'I have fought the fight the right way.' He means, 'I have been fighting in the good fight.' You and I also have to do so—we are both in the good fight. We stand on victory ground, because our fight is under King Jesus, and King Jesus is Victor. He makes us more than conquerors."

I saw that the boy looked happy when I told him this about fighting while standing on victory ground.

> I have fought a good fight, I have finished my course, I have kept the faith.
>
> 2 Timothy 4:7

17

His Sheep

Some time ago, I visited a friend of mine. He was a man who had often helped me. When I could not understand something in the Bible, he told me what it meant. He knew a great deal. He knew the Lord. However, there was one strange thing—he was afraid to die.

Now I had heard that he was very ill, so I went to him, thinking that I must try to help him so that he would no longer be afraid to die. It was possible that that moment would soon come. It would be such a pity if he should be afraid, since he had known the Lord for such a long time. I prayed in my heart, "Oh, Lord Jesus, will You touch him, will You take away all fear from his heart?"

When I entered his room, he looked very happy. I asked him, "Are you a little better?"

"No," he said, "I'm very weak and I know that I must die. But what I'm so very happy about is that Jesus said, 'I give My sheep life eternal!' It is good He said it, for I cannot do anything myself. I am so tired that I cannot think properly, but I know that He will take care of me—even . . . even now. I cannot do it, but He is able."

How good it was to see that all the fear had disappeared. The Lord Himself takes care of His own. When there are moments that are difficult, we do not have to fear anything, for He is able to help us. He is faithful. He loves us.

Yes, He gives, and all that we have to do—is accept! Not one of our prayers is lost. All our prayers are kept in heaven.

Another angel came and stood at the altar, having a golden censer; and there was given unto him much incense, that he should offer it with the prayers of all saints upon the golden altar which was before the throne.

Revelation 8:3

18

Little Angel

In a children's hospital, I stood with my hand in a mother's hand. Her little girl had died. She looked like a little angel. On that little girl's dead face there was such an expression of peace!

"Oh, what joy it must be for that little child to be with Jesus! She will be so happy in heaven."

"I believe that, too," the mother said, "but Corrie, you don't know how wounded I am. I loved my little girl so very much. Why did the Lord take her away from me?"

"I do not know, but God knows. He understands you. He loves you and He loves that little girl."

There are moments when the suffering is so deep that one can hardly talk to a person. What a joy it is then to know that the Lord understands. No pit is so deep that the Lord is not deeper still. Underneath us are the everlasting arms—and the Lord understands.

> He shall cover thee with his feathers, and under his wings shalt thou trust: his truth shall be thy shield and buckler.
>
> Psalms 91:4

19

The Lost Sheep

Recently I met someone who had known the Lord for a long time, but she had turned away from Him. I sang to her, "What a Friend We Have in Jesus."

"I sang that song when I was in Sunday school," she said. "Yes, then I heard about the Lord Jesus every Sunday, but I have gone astray. I did not speak to Him and I did not listen to Him for many years. And now I'm so ill—what can I do?"

I told her of the good shepherd who had a hundred sheep and one of them had also gone astray. "It did not come home with the others. That shepherd left the ninety-nine at home and went to seek that one silly sheep that had lost its way. He found it, took it in his arms, and brought it home. He was very, very happy. So Jesus is on His way looking for you. Won't you let yourself be found by this wonderful Friend who is our Saviour? He is looking for you, and when you call Him, He will take you and carry you home. He will be so happy!"

She closed her eyes and thought about it. Then, opening her eyes again, she said, "Is it as simple as all that?"

"Yes, it is."

She folded her hands. "Lord Jesus, forgive me for having gone my own way. Take me in Your arms and take me back home. Amen."

He was so near that it was as if we heard Him say, ". . . him that cometh to me I will in no wise cast out" (John 6:37).

She looked up and smiled a very happy smile. "What a Friend we have in Jesus!"

20

Worry

"Oh, my children! My husband! How can they live without me?"

I was in a hospital in a large town in the United States, and my friend Ann was very ill. She knew it and she did not tell me about her suffering, but about the greatest worry she had. "Just imagine that I should die—who would take care of my family?" I held her hand in mine and just prayed for her. Then suddenly, I remembered a little poem.

> Said the Robin to the Sparrow:
> "I should really like to know
> Why these anxious human beings
> Rush around and worry so."
>
> Said the Sparrow to the Robin:
> "Friend, I think that it must be
> That they have no heavenly Father
> Such as cares for you and me."
> ELIZABETH CHENEY

The Bible tells us:

Look at the birds in the sky. They neither sow nor reap nor store away in barns and yet your heavenly Father feeds them.
See Luke 12:24

Aren't you much more valuable to Him than they are? Can any one of you, however much he worries, make himself an inch taller? And why do you worry about clothes? Consider how the flowers grow. They neither work nor weave, but I tell you that even Solomon in all his glory was never arrayed like one of these. Now, if God so clothes the flowers of the field which are alive today and discarded tomorrow, is He not much more likely to clothe you—you of little faith? Don't worry at all, then, about tomorrow. Tomorrow can take care of itself. One day's trouble is enough for one day.

I could easily understand that her children and her husband were reasons to worry about the future. However, our times are in God's hands, and He loves her family even more than she loved them. Worrying is carrying tomorrow's load with today's strength—carrying two days at once. It is moving into tomorrow ahead of time. Worrying does not empty tomorrow of its sorrow—it empties today of its strength.

"Do you know, Ann, I do not believe that worry is from the Lord. It is from the enemy. There has been a man upon the earth of whom Satan is afraid, a man whom he can neither touch nor resist—Jesus Christ. And that is why we can go to Him for help. You are not able to overcome worry, but the Lord Jesus can, and He will—through His Holy Spirit. When we see that worry is a sin—and that is what it really is, for the Bible tells us not to worry—then we know what to do with sin, don't we?"

"Yes, we take it to the Lord, and when we confess our sins, the blood of Jesus cleanses us from all of our sins."

"That is true, so just ask forgiveness for having worried, and then ask Jesus to keep worry away. He gives us peace under all circumstances. I have a little stick here that cannot stand on my hand by itself. But I can even let it stand on the top of my finger, if my hand holds it. In the same way, we cannot keep worry away, but when we surrender to the wounded hands of Jesus, He keeps us from falling. One day He will present us blameless and with unspeakable joy. That will be on the day when He will reveal Himself. Jesus is stronger than all of our problems."

I prayed with Ann and then she said, "I have much to think about and I know one thing—I am not able, but Jesus is. He will do the job."

> Cast thy burden upon the Lord, and he shall sustain thee: he shall never suffer the righteous to be moved.
>
> Psalms 55:22

21

Our Times Are in God's Hands

It is a feast for me to be in Holland, for I meet friends of former days. I gather them in my home to tell them how much I have experienced during the last year. At one of these gatherings, I missed one of my friends. Somebody told me, "She is ill, so she could not come."

I went to see her. She told me what had happened. "I have been very ill, and everyone—myself, too—thought I had to die. Oh, Corrie, I was not afraid. I was just thinking about the joy of seeing the Lord Jesus as I read in the Bible all the promises that speak of heaven. But then I began to recover. I am not strong, but the doctor said that in a short while I shall be able to do my work again."

"Are you happy?"

"Yes. I can be an eternity in heaven and there is much work for me to do here in this world. I believe I will return to my everyday life richer than I was before I was ill. I see now that our times are in God's hands. I believe I will take the good opportunities, which the Lord will give me in the future, with more thankfulness, because I had thought I had lost them forever. I knew, when I was dying, how serious my condition was, but the Lord gave me grace. I was not afraid.

Now I know, as I go back to my everyday life, that I will see the smaller problems in the light of eternity. I am sure I will not be so concerned about the problems of everyday life. I thank God that I had this illness. It made me more ready for life."

> All things work together for good to them that love God. . . .
> Romans 8:28

The Lord never makes a mistake. One day, when we are in heaven, I'm sure we shall see the answers to the *whys*. My, how often I have asked, *"Why?"* In heaven we shall see God's side of the embroidery. God has no problems—only plans. There is never panic in heaven.

22

When I Saw Death

When I heard that my father had died in prison, I was alone in a cell. The prisoner who had been in the cell before me had written on the wall NOT LOST, BUT GONE BEFORE.

After the first shock, I realized what a great joy it was for Father to be with the Lord in the beautiful place that Jesus had prepared for him. Straight from the cell in a prison to that place of peace and love of God. I could thank the Lord that He had taken him home. Yes, he was not lost but gone before.

When I saw Betsie after she had died in the ward of the concentration camp, I saw an expression of intense joy and peace on her face. She even looked young. I could only thank and praise the Lord that He had taken her to Himself. It was as if her face reflected a little bit of the tremendous joy that her soul experienced at that moment, when she went to be with the Lord.

I looked death in the eyes several times myself, and when fear came into my heart I told the Lord Jesus. He did not give me a spirit of fear, but of power and of love and of a sound mind. I knew that I did not have to pass through the valley of the shadow of death alone. Jesus was with me.

The moment I was almost sure that death was coming was when my number was called out when we were standing on roll call. I had to stand as number one in the front row. Many of us thought—also I myself—that we had been called out because they were going to kill us.

I stood there for three hours, and next to me was a Dutch girl I had never seen before. I said to myself: "This is now the last person on earth to whom I can bring the Gospel." And I did. She told me her life story. I told her that Jesus loved her and that He had given His life on the cross to bear her punishment. That girl said *yes* to Jesus.

I was not killed, I was set free.

What do you think about death, about the death of your loved ones, and of yourself? Study the Bible, the answer is there. Talk with the Lord, He understands and loves you. When you come to Him, He will in no wise cast you out or send you away. Are you afraid? Give your fear to Him.

23

Are You Afraid to Die?

In Chicago I met an old friend of mine. I had not seen him for a long time, and I was spending only one day in his town. We had a good talk together, and I remember that I asked him a question. "Are you afraid to die?"

"Yes, I am," he said.

His answer surprised me. He loved the Lord and had known Him a long time. He had a deep faith in God. "Why are you afraid to die? You have been a Christian as long as I have known you. Surely you know that Jesus will not leave you alone for one moment."

"I am afraid, Corrie, because I have never died before. I am afraid because I do not know what it is like to die."

Then we talked about Jesus. Before He went to the cross, He had never died either. Was He also a little afraid?

But today Jesus knows what it is like to die. He has already been through death, and today Jesus says to you and to me, "I will never leave you nor forsake you," and "Lo, I am with you always." That means *even* death.

The old man smiled and said, "Isn't God good to us—that we could talk and think together about this today?"

"Are you afraid to die?"

Fear thou not; for I am with thee: be not dismayed; for I am thy God: I will strengthen thee; . . . yea, I will uphold thee with the right hand of my righteousness.

Isaiah 41:10

No temptation has overtaken you that is not common to man. God is faithful, and he will not let you be tempted beyond your strength, but with the temptation will also provide the way of escape, that you may be able to endure it.

1 Corinthians 10:13 RSV

"Are You Going Home?"

Are you going Home to be with the Lord?
You are not afraid, are you?

Afraid of what?
To feel the Spirit's glad release,
to pass from pain to perfect peace,
the strife and strain of life to cease?
Afraid of that?

Afraid of what?
Afraid to see the Saviour's face?
To hear His welcome and to trace
the glory gleam from wounds of grace?
Afraid of that?

Afraid of what?
To enter into heaven's rest
and yet, to serve the Master blessed,
from service good to service best?
Afraid of that?

Think of stepping on shore and finding it heaven, or taking hold of a hand and finding it God's, or breathing new air and finding it celestial, or feeling invigorated and finding it immortality; of passing through a tempest to a new and unknown ground; of waking up well and happy and finding it home.

You Have His Word

My sheep hear my voice, and I know them, and they follow me: And I give unto them eternal life; and they shall never perish, neither shall any man pluck them out of my hand.

John 10:27, 28

I am the resurrection and the life: He who believes in me will live, even though he dies.

John 11:25 NIV

The gift of God is eternal life through Jesus Christ our Lord.

Romans 6:23

Blessed be the God and Father of our Lord Jesus Christ, which according to his abundant mercy hath begotten us again unto a lively hope by the resurrection of Jesus Christ from the dead, To an inheritance incorruptible, and undefiled, and that fadeth not away, reserved in heaven for you.

1 Peter 1:3, 4

What we suffer now is nothing compared to the glory he will give us later.

Romans 8:18 LB

No mere man has ever seen, heard or even imagined what wonderful things God has ready for those who love the Lord.

1 Corinthians 2:9 LB

If we confess our sins, he is faithful and just to forgive us our sins, and to cleanse us from all unrighteousness.

1 John 1:9

Forasmuch as ye know that ye were not redeemed with corruptible things, as silver and gold, from your vain conversation received by tradition from your fathers; But with the precious blood of Christ, as of a lamb without blemish and without spot.

1 Peter 1:18, 19

But God commendeth his love toward us, in that, while we were yet sinners, Christ died for us.

Romans 5:8

Verily, verily, I say unto you, He that heareth my word, and believeth on him that sent me, hath everlasting life, and shall not come into condemnation; but is passed from death unto life.

John 5:24

These things have I written unto you that believe on the name of the Son of God; that ye may know that ye have eternal life, and that ye may believe on the name of the Son of God.

1 John 5:13

For our light affliction, which is but for a moment, worketh for us a far more exceeding and eternal weight of glory.

2 Corinthians 4:17

For we know that if our earthly house of this tabernacle were dissolved, we have a building of God, a house not made with hands, eternal in the heavens.

2 Corinthians 5:1

But thanks be to God, which giveth us the victory through our Lord Jesus Christ.

1 Corinthians 15:57

Part Two

He Sets
the
Captive Free

Preface

I know how it feels to be behind a door that can be opened only from the outside, for I have been a prisoner in three different prisons. I learned a great deal in prison, as this was a very difficult class in the schoolroom of life. When you are in a difficult class with a good teacher, you learn much—and my teacher was very good. It was Jesus Himself!

I wish I could share with you what I learned during my imprisonment, but I am old and I cannot travel much now. Since we cannot speak personally together, I have decided to visit you through this little book. The conversations, the experiences really happened to me and I want to share them with you—to show you that even when circumstances look utterly bleak, there is a victorious life which is real and available to you.

It is not only behind barbed wire or prison doors that there are prisoners. There are prisoners of sin, of lust, prisoners of wrong philosophies, prisoners of circumstances, prisoners of *self*. There are prisoners everywhere. I pray that this book will help you too to lose your life for Jesus' sake so that you may gain it. Jesus said that those whom He makes free are free indeed. Whether decent or indecent sinners, we all need Jesus. He loves us. Yes, He loves you!

1

I Was in Prison

"Name?" the Interrogator inquired.

"Cornelia ten Boom, and . . . ."

"Age?"

"Fifty-two."

It was a dark night when we were finally marched out of the building. We could see before us a large canvas-roofed army truck. The truck had no springs and we bounced roughly over the bomb-pitted streets of The Hague. Leaving the downtown section, we seemed to be headed west, toward the suburbs of Scheveningen. Now we knew our destination; the Federal Penitentiary named after this seaside town of Scheveningen.

We turned left into an endless world of steel and concrete.

"Ten Boom, Cornelia!"

Another door rasped open. The cell was deep and narrow, scarcely wider than the door. A woman lay on the single cot, three others on straw ticks on the floor. "Give this one the cot," the matron said. "She's sick."

Soon I was moved to another location. The cell was identical to the one I had just left: six steps long, two wide, a single cot at the back. But this cell was empty. As the guard's footsteps died away down the corridor, I leaned against the cold metal of the door. Alone. Alone behind these walls . . . solitary!

Weeks later, "Get your things together! Get ready to evacuate!" The shouts of the guards echoed up and down the long corridor. I was thankful to see other faces again, . . . but!

Where would we be taken? Where were we headed? One thing I dreaded . . . please . . . not into Germany!

Hours passed as the loaded train sat on the siding. It must have been two or three in the morning when the train at last began to move. The thought uppermost in every mind was: Is it Germany?

Finally we seemed to stop in the middle of a wood. Floodlights mounted in trees lit a broad rough-cleared path lined by soldiers with leveled guns.

Spurred on by the shouts of the guards, I started up the path between the gun barrels. "Close ranks! Keep up! Five abreast!"

The nightmare march lasted a mile or more, when at last we came to a barbed-wire fence surrounding a row of wooden barracks. We went into one of them and fell into an exhausted sleep. So began our stay in this place that we learned was named Vught, after the nearest small village. Vught had been constructed in Holland by the occupation army primarily as a concentration camp for political prisoners.

Several months later we were moved to another camp. After a night punctuated with the hail of bullets and machine-gun fire, we learned at dawn that we were passing through a border town into Germany. For two more incredible days and nights we were carried deeper and deeper into the land of our fears.

From the crest of the hill, we saw a vast scar on the green German landscape; a city of low gray barracks, surrounded by concrete walls on which guard towers rose at intervals. In the very center a square smokestack emitted a thin gray vapor into the blue sky.

"Ravensbruck!"

Like a whispered curse, the word passed back through the lines. This was the notorious extermination camp for women, whose name we had heard even in Holland.

Adapted from *The Hiding Place*

2

Why I Was Sent to Prison

I want to tell you about my experiences in three prisons. During World War II, I was a prisoner of the Gestapo because my family, my friends, and I had saved the lives of Jewish people in Holland. Adolf Hitler was preparing to kill all of them, and our task was to help them to escape to safer countries.

When that was no longer possible, we hid them in our houses. In the end we had a group of eighty people with whom we worked to supply the desperate needs of a hidden people: food, clothing, houses, burials. There were many other factors facing a group of helpless persons hiding in a country already stripped by the occupying army of a powerful enemy.

We were betrayed and all were arrested. My father was eighty-four years old, and lived only a short while in the prison where all his children and a grandson were also incarcerated. We never saw him again, for the prison walls separated us.

Father was a courageous man, but he understood that he was too old for prison life. "If I am imprisoned, I shall die, but it will be an honor for me to give my life for God's chosen people, the Jews," he said before they arrested him. I heard much later that he had died after only ten days' imprisonment.

3

Solitary Confinement

For the first week, they put me in a cell with four or five others, for I was very ill with pleurisy. The prison doctor said it would develop into tuberculosis, so I was sent to solitary confinement. He didn't want me to infect the others.

For the first time ever, I was really alone, and I knew my life was completely in the hands of the enemy. They could kill me or torture me or just forget about me altogether, and there would be no one to know or care.

At night the sounds of distant bombing penetrated the thick walls—and from somewhere within came the muffled cries of people being tortured by the Gestapo—that was a little bit of hell! When I lost courage, I tried singing, but the guards pounded on the door and demanded silence. They threatened to take me to the *dark* cell. In the dark cell you had to stand in water. Time became a very thick thing that I struggled to wade through.

Solitary confinement lasted four months. It wasn't only the isolation that was so hard, but the constant threat that at any moment of the day or night they would come for me. Whenever I heard footsteps outside my cell I would ask myself, "Are they coming to torture or kill me?"

Once I stood with my back against the wall with my hands spread out, as if to try to push away the walls that were closing in on me. I was dead scared. I cried out, "Lord, I'm not strong enough to endure this. I don't have the faith!"

Suddenly I noticed an ant which I had watched roaming the floor of the cell for days. I had just mopped the floor with a wet rag, and the moment the ant felt the water on the stones, he ran straight to his tiny hole in the wall.

Then it was as if the Lord said to me, "What about that ant? He didn't stop to look at the wet rag or his weak feet— he went straight to his hiding place. Corrie, don't look at your faith; it is weak, like the tiny feet of that ant. Don't dwell on the treatment you might receive from these cruel people. I am your hiding place, and you can come running to Me just like that ant disappeared into that hole in the wall."

That brought real peace into my heart. I was then fifty-three years old, and I had always known about Jesus, but there in solitary confinement I began to really understand and experience for myself that His light is stronger than the deepest darkness.

I know there are moments for you when you lose all courage. You feel as a prisoner that you don't exist in the eyes of the people around you, in the eyes of God, or in your own eyes. Then you can read in the Bible a promise from Jesus: "Come to Me, all you who have heavy burdens, and I will give you rest" (Matthew 11:28). When you can believe that, you will *know* Someone is still interested in you. Someone still cares about you—not as a number, but as a person.

4

The Interrogation

After two months in the cell, I was called in for interrogation. The judges, the *Sachbearbeiters*, had a tremendous amount of power, and you had no rights whatever. They could give you a short sentence, a long sentence, or sentence you to death. You were totally in their hands.

I will never forget the moment when I was brought before my judge. I knew that not only my own life was in his hands, but that I could incriminate many friends and co-workers. If I were forced to tell about them, it could mean their death sentence, too.

I prayed for wisdom to answer all the questions of the interrogator, and there were *many* questions! I had to give my whole life history, even what I did in my spare time.

I told him that I taught a Bible class for feebleminded people who could not go to church because they could not understand sermons. "They need the Lord Jesus just as much as you and I do," I said to this National Socialist judge.

He replied, "What a waste of time! Isn't there far more value in converting a normal person than an abnormal one?"

My answer was, "If you knew Jesus, you would know that He has a great love for everyone who is despised or in need. It is possible that a poor, feebleminded child has more value in His eyes than you and I together."

He was angry when I said that, and he called the policemen, saying, "Take her back to her cell."

The next day I was brought again before my judge, who said, "I could not sleep during the night. I was thinking over what you had said about Jesus. I don't know anything about Him. We have plenty of time for the interrogation. First, tell me what you know about Jesus."

Boy, was that an opportunity! I began, "Jesus is a light come into this world. No one who believes in Him remains in darkness. Is there darkness in your life?"

His answer was, "Darkness? There is no light at all in my life. I hate my work. My wife is in Bremen, Germany. I don't even know if she is still alive. The town is being bombed heavily every night now. It is possible that she was killed this very night."

Suddenly the contact between us was on a totally different level. He was no longer the judge, but simply a man in great need, and I, his prisoner, could give him real encouragement as I brought him the Gospel.

I said to him, "Jesus once said, 'Come to me, all who are heavy laden, and I will give you rest.' Come to me—*all*. That means you, too. Come unto Jesus and He will give you rest. Tell Him your sins. He has never sent away any sinner."

I had a good talk with that man, and from then on he was no longer my enemy, but my friend. He helped to save my life and did his utmost, though unsuccessfully, to set me free.

Of course, he still had to do his job, and so he showed me papers found in my house. To my horror I saw names, addresses, and particulars which could mean not only *my* death sentence but the death of my family and my friends as well.

"Can you explain these papers?" he asked.

"No, I cannot." I felt miserable. (You will say, "Why did you have such dangerous papers in your house?" In our underground efforts to save Jewish people, I worked with many young people who did remarkably courageous work. But they were not always careful, so these papers were found in my house.)

The judge knew even better than I how dangerous those papers were. Suddenly he turned around, opened the door of the stove, and threw all the papers into the stove. At that moment it was as if I understood for the first time the text in Colossians 2:13, 14 PHILLIPS:

> . . . God has now made [you] to share in the very life of Christ! He has forgiven you all your sins: Christ has utterly wiped out the damning evidence of broken laws and commandments which always hung over our heads, and has completely annulled it by nailing it over His own Head on the Cross.

In heaven there are dangerous papers for us all, and whether we believe it or not, we will have to come before the judgment seat of God. If we have refused Jesus Christ in this life, then the Judgment Day will be terrible. But if we have received Jesus as our Saviour and Lord, then we have nothing to fear, because Jesus nailed these terrible papers to the cross when He died for the sins of the whole world—your sins and mine. That is what I understood when I saw those papers destroyed by the flames in that stove.

Years later I met that judge in Germany, and I asked him, "Did you bring your sins to Him? It says in the Bible, 'If you confess your sins, He is faithful and just to forgive you, and He will cleanse you from all unrighteousness.' "

His answer was, "No, I did not do that. I am a very good man, and I have never committed sins."

"I am sorry you think that, because that means you cannot have salvation. Jesus will never ever send away anybody who comes to Him. But there is one kind of person in the Bible that I must tell you about.

"That was the Pharisee who said, 'I am good.' And Jesus could not and would not help him. If the time comes when you know you have sins, that you are a sinner, don't forget what I told you. The Bible tells us that Jesus has accepted our punishment at the cross, and the only thing we have to do is to receive Him as our Saviour and come to Him and confess our sins."

He thought a moment and then suddenly said, "I know a sin that I have done."

I said, "All right—bring it to the Lord at once. Ask His forgiveness and thank Him for His forgiveness." He did.

Later in the evening he said, "I see another sin in my life."

"So, you know that you are a sinner. That is good. Just bring it to the Lord and ask forgiveness," I replied. When for the *fourth* time he remembered a sin which needed to be brought to the Lord, I knew he was ready to receive the Lord Jesus Christ as his Saviour.

I said, "Now you can accept Jesus. You know that you need Him."

He did, and I know that his sins were forgiven and that his name was written in the Book of Life.

5

Ravensbruck

The Nazis were emptying jails everywhere! Male prisoners were sent in one division, and women prisoners in another. My sister Betsie and I, herded together with thousands of other women, were marched into Ravensbruck. It was called a work camp.

When we first came into this concentration camp, they took all our possessions. It was a real miracle that I was able to keep my Bible.

At great risk, I hid it on my back under my dress, and I prayed, "Lord, will You send Your angels to surround me?" Then I thought, *But angels are spirits, and you can see through spirits. I don't want these people to see me!* so I prayed then, in great fear, "Let Your angels *not* be transparent. Let them cover me."

And God did it! As we passed through the inspection, the woman in front of me was searched, then my sister, directly behind me, was searched—but I walked through unsearched!

Our barracks was built for four hundred women, but they packed fourteen hundred of us inside. Bunks were stacked all the way to the ceiling, and we each had a sleeping space only a few inches wide. When they were all working, we had eight toilets for the entire barracks!

In Ravensbruck it was dangerous to use the Word of God. If you were caught teaching the Bible, you were killed in a cruel way, but the guards never knew that I had a Bible meeting twice each day in Barracks 28. The one jammed room was filthy, crawling with fleas and lice, and the guards never came inside the door. You see how the Lord used both angels and lice to keep my Bible in our possession?

6

Does He Forget Me?

Sometimes I experienced moments of great despair. I remember one night when I was outside the barracks on my way to roll call. The stars were beautiful. I remember saying, "Lord, You guide all those stars. You have not forgotten them but You have forgotten Betsie and me."

Then Betsie said: "No, He has not forgotten us. I know that from the Bible. The Lord Jesus said, 'I am with you always, until the end of the world,' and Corrie, He is here with us. We must believe that. It is not what we are *feeling* that counts, but what we believe!"

Feelings come and feelings go
And feelings are deceiving.
My warrant is the Word of God,
None else is worth believing.

I slowly learned not to trust in myself or my faith or my feelings, but to trust in Him. Feelings come and go—they are deceitful. In all that hell around us, the promises from the Bible kept us sane.

Ravensbruck certainly *was* a work camp. It was the enemy's plan to work us—to death! Before the war ended, ninety-six thousand women died there. Even my dear Betsie became an old woman before my eyes and slowly starved to death.

The smoke from the crematorium was like a black haze over the camp. Every day seven hundred women died or were killed. There were far too many of us, and death was the only solution to the problem. I looked death in the eye day after day, and I found the Lord to be my refuge still, my only hiding place.

7

The Lifeline

The greatest moment of your life can be when everything seems finished for you. That is the moment when you lay your weak hand in the strong hand of Jesus. For Jesus can make life and death—present and future—victorious! He can give you eternal life; not only life in heaven, but life right now.

It is as when you have fallen in the sea and you think: *Now I will surely drown. I can swim perhaps an hour, but then I will sink!* A lifeline is the only thing that can help you then.

I found that when you are drowning in the terrific misery of the world, Jesus is everything for you—your only lifeline. When you think you have lost everything, then you can be *found* by Jesus Christ.

He died for you. He lives for you, and He loves you more than any human being can love. I have told people about Him for thirty-three years, in sixty-four countries, and in all that time nobody has ever told me he was sorry he asked Jesus to come into his life. You won't be sorry, either.

8

A Storm Laid Down

Punishments were often general in Ravensbruck. Once we suddenly heard shouting, beating, and swearing in our room. We lived in a crowded room, packed together. Everything was filthy and broken-down. Two people were sharing a very small bunk, and one had thrown the other out of the cot, so they started to fight.

Betsie said, "Corrie, we need to pray. This is dangerous!"

It *was* dangerous. If the guards had heard the fighting in our barracks, we would all have been cruelly punished. Betsie remained praying. She prayed and prayed. It was as if a storm died down. We heard less beating, less swearing and shouting. Finally, it was quiet, and Betsie said, "Thank You, Father. A*men.*"

Now, do you see what happened there? There was a room with many prisoners in great danger, and there was one starving old woman—Betsie. God used Betsie to save the situation. That is what God is willing to do and is going to do with you and me when we let Him show us what to do— when He guides us.

The Bible says that we are representatives of heaven on this earth; that we are ambassadors of Jesus Christ. It is terribly important for the world that there are ambassadors—representatives from heaven—in this world, and you and I can be those ambassadors. Often it will save the situation and bless our surroundings. Because we do it so well? No, not at all. Because the Lord is using us to do what *He* wants done.

9

No Wilderness, the Lord's Garden

"You must tickle the hand of God before He is willing to help you," said a prisoner who was sitting on the bed behind me.

"No, girl, that is not true. When you really know the Lord, you know that He is far more ready to bless us than we are ready to ask for His blessing. He loves us. The Bible says, 'You are God's field' " (*see* 1 Corinthians 3:9 RSV). The great preacher and writer C. H. Spurgeon expresses this very clearly:

> Oh, to have one's soul as a field under
>   heavenly cultivation,
> No wilderness, but a garden of the Lord,
>   walled around by grace,
> Planted by instruction, visited by love,
> Weeded by heavenly discipline, guarded by
>   divine power.
> One's soul thus favored is prepared to yield
>   fruit unto the glory of God.

A garden does not do much. It does bring forth fruit and flowers. But the one who has the responsibility is the gardener, and it is He, our Gardener, who blesses us, surrounds us with grace, and disciplines us. Whether we are willing or not, He does the job. On our part it is necessary to surrender, and then He makes His garden from the wilderness of our lives. It is wonderful what He is willing and able to do.

10

Is Forgiveness Possible?

Do you know how it feels when your heart is full of hatred? We were working in an area where wrecked airplanes were piled together. We had to gather the many pieces and load them onto big trucks. It was terribly heavy work for us.

My sister Betsie was a very frail woman, and she could not lift much, but she did her utmost. Suddenly one of the guards noticed that Betsie was picking up only the little pieces, because the big pieces were too heavy for her.

Betsie said kindly to her, "Don't give me more to do than I am trying to do already, because I am not strong enough to lift these heavy parts."

The woman guard said, "You don't decide what you do. *I* decide." Suddenly the guard started to brutally beat Betsie. I have never been so enraged! The other prisoners held me back so I could not grab the guard.

When she had gone, I ran to Betsie, who had blood all over her face. She said, "No, don't hate, Corrie. You must love and forgive."

"I cannot! I am not able."

If there is hate in your heart, you cannot forgive. I knew this, and I also knew that Jesus had said:

> But if you do not forgive, neither will your
> Father who is in heaven forgive your trespasses.
>
> Mark 11:26

After we were back in our barracks, I climbed out of the window and went for a little walk alone, and I talked with the Lord. I said, "Lord, I cannot forgive that brutal woman. It is more difficult to forgive when people you love suffer than when you suffer yourself."

Then the Lord reminded me of a text. I had my little Bible hidden under my dress. I opened it and read:

> ... God's love has been poured into our hearts through the Holy Spirit which has been given to us.
>
> Romans 5:5 RSV

Suddenly I saw that what *I* was not able to do, the Lord, in me, was able to do. I said, "Oh, Lord, I thank You for Romans 5:5. I thank You, Jesus, that You brought into my heart God's love through the Holy Spirit. Thank You, Father, that Your love in me is stronger than my hatred."

At that moment, when I was able to forgive, my hatred disappeared. What a liberation! Forgiveness is the key which unlocks the door of resentment and the handcuffs of hatred. It is a power that breaks the chains of bitterness and the shackles of selfishness. What a liberation it is when you can forgive. Here again we see that we are not a wilderness, but a garden of the Lord, when we give our lives to Jesus. He does the job.

11

Lizzy

We had to live in beds stacked one on top of another. There were three beds in each stack, and above the cots where my sister Betsie and I slept, there lived a girl, Lizzy, who was a prostitute. Every day Betsie gathered the people around us, and she or I gave a little Bible talk. Lizzy did not join us, but she always listened, and once I heard Betsie talking with her.

"I do not know if I can come to Jesus," Lizzy said to Betsie.

"Why not? The Lord loves you. You are very precious in God's eyes, and when you come to Jesus, He will not send you away. He has never sent anyone away who came to seek forgiveness and to find the answer for his sin or guilt problem.

"God made this world good, and human beings were without sin, but then we people started to do wrong things, and God had to punish us. But He loved us so much that He had a talk with His Son, Jesus, and God said, 'What must I do? I have to punish people, but I love them.'

"Jesus said, 'Father, I will go to the world, and I will carry their punishment.' And the Father agreed. Jesus came to this world and He lived here for thirty-three years. That must have been a difficult time for Him, even from the beginning, for He was used to being in heaven, and then He came to such a dark world, full of problems.

"The most terrible thing He experienced was when He was crucified. Crucifixion is a very cruel, torturous way to kill people. He could have been saved from that. There were many angels around Him, and had Jesus told them to keep Him from the cross, they would have done so. But He did not ask them, because He was willing to suffer and die. It was His purpose, when He came into this world, to die for your sins and mine.

"Now when we believe in Him we do not have to fear any punishment. We are free! There will be a Judgment Day and every one of us will be present there, but we have nothing to fear when we believe in the Lord Jesus Christ. There is no condemnation for those who belong to Him. And Jesus Himself is our Judge and Advocate. You can read that in the Bible."

> Who then will condemn us? Will Christ? No! For he is the one who died for us and came back to life again for us and is sitting at the place of highest honor next to God, pleading for us there in heaven.
>
> Romans 8:34 LB

"But I don't do what I should do!" said Lizzy.

"I don't believe that you must do anything," replied Betsie. "Believe in the Lord Jesus Christ and you will be saved. What had to be done has all been done by Jesus Christ. Your part is to accept that at the cross He died for your sins."

Lizzy folded her hands and said, "Thank You, Jesus, that You did it all at the cross. I surely am not able to do much to change myself, but I thank You that You will do it in me."

12

The Red Ticket

"Fall in for the street commando!"

Making streets was heavy work. Betsie and I showed our red tickets, which we had just received from the *Aufseherin*. They were the sign that we were unable to do hard labor. We climbed on our cot and hummed a little song. We picked up the stockings, which we had to knit for the German soldiers.

"You seem to be happy," said the woman behind us.

"We certainly are. We were called to enroll in the street commando, and look what we have." We showed the red tickets.

The woman smiled cynically. "Do you know what your red tickets mean? At the first cleaning up of prisoners, all the red-ticket owners disappear into the gas chamber."

We stopped humming our song. I looked through the window at the smoke which was going up from the crematorium and I thought, "When will my time come to be killed?"

Betsie saw what I was looking at. "Are you afraid, Corrie?"

Afraid? Of what?
To feel the Spirit's glad release?
To pass from pain to perfect peace?
The strife and strain of life to cease?
Afraid of that?

I knew that my sins were forgiven, that my name was in the Book of Life, and that I had received Jesus as my Saviour. He had made me a child of God. Jesus gives eternal life. That means the life that belongs to eternity, to heaven. And I had that.

I knew that if they killed me I would go to the Father's house with many mansions. I looked death in the eyes. I saw the valley of the shadow of death. But I was not afraid, for I knew that I would not go alone through that valley. Jesus was going to take my hand and help me through.

How good to know that you belong to Jesus! Do you know it? If not, lay your hand in His strong hand. Those who come to Him, He will in no wise cast out.

13

Ask More—He Will Give

It was crowded and filthy and miserable in that room built for two hundred where seven hundred of us lived together. (There were two such rooms.) Although it was a terrible place, yet there were several things for which I was thankful.

One reason for gratitude was that twice a day Betsie or I could gather the prisoners around us for a little Bible message. First I did it only on Sunday, but when I saw that so many people died or were killed from one Sunday to the next, I decided to risk it every day.

Several of my fellow prisoners really came to the Lord and accepted the Lord Jesus as their Saviour. They decided to come every day for the Bible message. Then I gave the talk in the evenings for those prisoners who were assigned to work elsewhere during the day and couldn't attend the daytime meetings in the area where I had to knit stockings.

When I finished teaching, there would be many questions, and I realized that many did not know the simplest truths of the Bible.

I often talked about the fact that when we pray, the Lord hears our prayers. He loves us and loves to have us talk to Him. He always listens when we pray. I told them about the miracles that actually happened to me when God answered my prayers. Sometimes He does not answer our prayers in the way we want or expect Him to answer. We will understand why one day when we are in heaven.

I told them the story of a blind man who came to Jesus during the time that Jesus was in the world with us. Jesus healed him, and then He asked the man, "Can you see?"

The man said, "I see men like trees walking." Jesus touched his eyes again, and the man said "Now I can see clearly." (Read this in Mark 8:23–25.)

You know, sometimes when you first come to Jesus, it is as if you do not see so very much and you do not understand what is happening. You are not able to enjoy your new life. Then the best thing you can do is to tell the Lord that you do not understand it, that you do not see clearly, and that you really see man as the blind man did—like walking trees.

If Jesus had not asked this blind man whether he could see, I am sure that nevertheless the man would have told Him, and said, "Lord, I am glad that I can see a little bit, but I do not see enough." Then Jesus would have healed him.

So it is with you and me. If we do not see as much as we need or want to see, then we must tell it to the Lord. He will heal our eyes so that we see that the love of God is far greater than anything else.

There is an ocean of God's love which we discover when we receive Jesus Christ as our Saviour. He shows it to us through His Holy Spirit. God sees you and me. He knows everything about us, and He loves us so much that He wants to help us and do what we ask.

14

Is a *No* Answer an Answer?

When God gives us the *no* answer, it can be a difficult testing of our faith, but when we study the Bible, we understand more and more that God never makes a mistake. Once we are in heaven, we will understand it all.

> My life is like a weaving between my God and me,
> I do not choose the colors, He worketh steadily.
> Ofttimes He weaveth sorrow and I in foolish pride,
> Forget He sees the upper, and I the underside.

I once prayed for Betsie, my sister. She was so *very* ill. Even in the filthy bunk in our barrack or at our work, it was such a joy and comfort for us just to be together night and day. Now she was in that primitive hospital, and our friends and I, who loved her so, prayed that the Lord would heal her. But when I returned to the hospital after roll call and looked through the window, I saw that she had died. That was one of the darkest moments of my life.

I could not understand why God had not answered my prayer. A few days later, I was called out of lineup and I heard that I was to be set free. I had to go through the office on my way out, and I learned that they did not know my sister had died. I asked them, "What about my sister?" I wanted to find out what would have happened to her if she had still been alive.

They said, "Your sister must remain here for the duration of the war."

"May I remain with my sister?"

"Not for a minute! Now get out!"

I have praised and thanked my Lord for that unanswered prayer. Just imagine how it would have been if she had been healed, and would have had to stay in the hell of Ravensbruck without me. I would have returned to my homeland tormented night and day by the consciousness of her suffering. I saw God's side of the embroidery.

15

Freedom

It was 3:30 A.M. I woke up, and my first thought was, *Roll call.* I looked around me. Clean windows, a chair, a table a picture on the wall. I was no longer in prison. I was free!

I could sleep for several more hours but I did not. I got up and started to write down what I had experienced in the three prisons. Those writings became my first book, A *Prisoner and Yet . . . .* It became a best seller in Holland, because people were interested in reading about what had happened to the victims of the concentration camps.

For many years of my life I had been the leader of Girl Guide clubs (European Girl Scouts). As soon as I recovered my strength a bit, I got together with all the girls I could locate to tell them what I had experienced, and to find out what had happened to them.

After much talk together, they asked, "What are you going to do?" We were sitting in a clubhouse, cross-legged on the floor. My club girls were interested in all I had learned in prison—that difficult class in life's school.

"Girls, I'm so thankful that all my tomorrows are in God's hands. I want to tell you what happened one night." And this was what I told them:

It was midnight in Ravensbruck, and Betsie tried to wake me up. Sleep was such an important thing. You forgot that you were in prison.

"Why are you waking me up? Leave me, please, in the world of dreams, where there are no guards, no barbed wire, and no lice."

Betsie put her coat over our heads so that we could talk without disturbing our fellow prisoners. "I have to talk with you, Corrie. God has told me several things which we must do after the war, and I am afraid that I may forget some of His instructions.

"We have learned so much here, and now we must go all over the world to tell people what we now know—that Jesus' light is stronger than the deepest darkness. Only prisoners can know how desperate this life is. We can tell from experience that no pit is too deep, because God's everlasting arms always sustain us.

"We must rent a concentration camp after the war, where we can help displaced Germans to get a roof over their heads. I have heard that ninety-five percent of the houses in Germany are bombed out. No one will want these concentration camps after the war, so we must rent one and help the German people find a new life in a destroyed Germany. God has shown me in a vision, a house in Holland in which we will receive the Dutch prisoners who survive the concentration camps. We will help them to find their way through life again."

I asked her, "Must we stay in that camp which we will open for the people here in Germany, or will we be able to stay in the house for the ex-prisoners, at home in Holland?"

"Neither," Betsie said. "You must travel all over the world and tell everybody who will listen what we have learned here—that Jesus is a reality and that He is stronger than all the powers of darkness. Tell them. Tell everyone who will listen! He is our greatest Friend, our hiding place."

A week later Betsie died. A week after that I was set free,

and only one week later, the Germans put to death all the women of my age in Ravensbruck.

I looked at my Girl Guides who had listened to my story. "Girls," I said, "I know that you are sincerely interested in what I am going to do. My answer is that I will obey all the instructions that God gave to me through Betsie."

I obeyed. You can read about many of my adventures over the years in my book *Tramp for the Lord.*

Since I have often visited in prisons, now I want to talk with you about some of these experiences.

16

Kimio

While visiting a prison in Africa, I heard about a young man who was sentenced to die. I asked to see him, but the prison officials would allow me to enter his cell only if three soldiers went in with me.

The cell had a very high ceiling and one small window at the top for light. It was bare, except for a shelf very low to the ground. Sitting on that shelf was a handsome black African who had one more week to live. I was praying very hard! I wanted to be able to talk with him as if we were alone, but the soldiers made me uncomfortable. I always reacted that way when I was around men with guns.

As we talked, I learned that the young man's name was Kimio and that he had a wife and children. Kimio knew about the cross, and that Jesus had died there for the sins of the whole world, including his sins.

I asked him if he knew who was responsible for his arrest and imprisonment. He was a political prisoner, and there came into his eyes the darkness of hatred.

"I can name every person responsible for my being here," he said.

"Can you forgive them?"

"No, I can't."

"I understand that. Once a man betrayed me and my whole family. Because of his betrayal, four of my family died in prison, and I suffered in three of the most horrible prisons in the whole world.

"And, Kimio, I could forgive that man. Not through my own strength—never—but through the Lord. The Holy Spirit can fill your heart with God's love, and He can give you the power to forgive. Kimio, I felt so free after I had forgiven that man. You have to die very soon."

"Yes, and I have a wife and children that I will never see again because of those men."

"I understand, Kimio, but you have to come before God. You have to face a righteous God very soon, and you know about Jesus at the cross.

"Jesus said, 'If you do not forgive those who wrong you, my heavenly Father will not forgive you.' So Kimio, you *have* to forgive.

"You are unable, but the Holy Spirit in you *is* able. Just pray this prayer with me. 'Thank You, Jesus, that You have brought into my heart God's love through the Holy Spirit. Thank You, Father, that Your love in me is stronger than my hatred.' "

I don't remember what else Kimio and I talked about after that, but I no longer felt the presence of those three armed soldiers. There was the presence of angels in that cell. I learned later that Kimio wrote to his wife: "Love the people who have brought me here. Forgive them. You can't, and I can't, but Jesus *in* us is able."

Kimio was trapped by the misery of this world, but he learned how to be free.

17

Joy? Is That Possible?

The worst prison I have ever seen was in another area of Africa. The building was too small for all the prisoners. Only half of them could go inside the building at night; the rest had to stay outside.

During the day they were all kept crammed together in the dirty compound in front of the prison. There had been a tropical rainstorm, and the ground was one large pool of mud. I saw that some men had branches on which they were sitting. Some had small pieces of paper, and others had little shelves. They had all struggled to find something to sit on. Everything was dark and black, but the darkest was the expression of their faces.

I often pray at the same time I am speaking, saying one thing to the Lord and another to the people who are listening to my talk. On this day I said, "Lord, give me a message for these men that will help them in this very difficult place where they live."

The answer from the Lord was, "What is the fruit of the Spirit?" I knew it:

> The fruit of the Spirit is love, joy, peace, long-suffering, gentleness, goodness, faith.
>
> See Galatians 5:22 RSV

Then the Lord said, "Speak about joy."

"Lord, how can I speak about joy to these people who live in this terrible place?"

The answer was, "My Holy Spirit is here in this place, and the fruit of the Spirit is available wherever you are."

Then I remembered that when I had been in prison I had found joy even in the midst of the most desperate surroundings. When we are powerless to do a thing, it is a great joy that we can come and step inside the ability of Jesus.

"Lord," I said, "You are able to give joy." Then I heard myself giving a very happy message. The faces of the men lit up when I told them that the joy of the Lord can be our strength, even when we are in very difficult circumstances.

The only thing necessary to begin moving into the joy of the Lord is to tell Jesus Christ that you would like to be His follower. "Receive Jesus Christ as your Saviour and Lord, and He will give you the joy," I said.

Many did. I could see it in their faces. But I also saw faces of people who were not ready or willing. They remained just as dark and unhappy as before.

I said to them, "Fellows, I can understand that you think such joy is not possible for you when you are in this prison, but I can tell you that I was in a prison far worse than yours, where only twenty percent of us came out alive. The rest all starved or were killed in a cruel way. But the Lord Jesus was with us. His Holy Spirit was in our hearts, and there was often a great joy.

"There is joy for you, too, but you must be at peace with God and man—that *is* possible! When you confess your sins to the Lord, He is faithful and just, and He forgives you. He removes your sins, He cleanses your heart, and He fills you with the Holy Spirit. The fruit of the Spirit is joy."

Finally I asked, "Who is willing to receive Jesus Christ? Raise your hand."

All the prisoners did, and even the guards who were there did, too! Now, when *everyone* raises his hand to accept Jesus

Christ, then I do not always trust it, but I looked into their faces and saw that this time it was real for all of them.

When I went to the car to leave for the next place, all the men and the guards accompanied me to the street. They were standing around the car, shouting something which I could not understand. I asked the missionary who was with me, "What are these men saying?"

She smiled and said, "They are shouting, 'Come again, old woman. Come again and tell us more about Jesus.' "

I was so glad! You know, I had to leave, but the Lord stayed with these men, and the Holy Spirit filled their hearts. It is true that when you lay your weak hand in the strong hand of Jesus, He keeps you from falling and never leaves you alone.

18

Three Decent Sinners

The Apostle Paul was in prison. It must have been terrible for him. His hands were chained to the hands of two guards night and day. He never knew from one day to the next what the enemy was intending to do with him.

We do know some of the things that Paul did while a prisoner. He wrote letters, which you should read. Some of these "epistles" you should read are called Ephesians, Philippians, Colossians, and the two letters to Timothy.

Another thing we know about Paul is that he used his time in prison to bring the Gospel to the people around him. These men to whom he was chained could not run away when he preached. And what was the result? People were converted! At the very end of his letter to the Philippian Church, Paul writes:

> Greetings to every true Christian, from me and all the brothers here with me. All the Christians here would like to send their best wishes, particularly those who belong to the Emperor's household.
>
> Philippians 4:21, 22 PHILLIPS

I once spoke about this in a prison in New Zealand, because I believe that every prisoner can help his fellow prisoners to know and receive Jesus Christ. Prisoners can be reached by their fellow prisoners better than by people from outside, because they understand one another.

I know some of you are thinking what some of the prisoners there in New Zealand thought: "Perhaps God can use other people, but not me. I am not good enough."

Do you know what happened there? One of the prisoners suddenly stood up and said, "Fellows, this morning I read in the Bible about three murderers. One's name was Paul, one was Moses, and the other was David. We know them as heroes of God, but all three were murderers. What God can do with a totally surrendered murderer! There is hope for you and me, fellows!"

Yes, there is hope for you who read this. I believe I have never heard such a good sermon as that one from a man who was a prisoner. What God can do with you when you surrender all is *tremendous!* There is one condition:

> Stay always within the boundaries where God's love can reach and bless you.
>
> Jude 21 LB

I have a glove. This glove cannot do anything, but when my hand is in the glove, the glove can do many things. It can drive a car, it can write.

Yes, I know, it is not the glove that does it, it is the hand inside the glove. You and I are—and Moses, David, and Paul were—just gloves. It was the Holy Spirit in them, and in you and me, who does the work.

What we have to do is to make room for the Holy Spirit, and then miracles can happen in our lives. Perhaps you think, "Oh, that is possible for a *mature* Christian, for somebody who knows the Bible well, and has had training." Perhaps you even think you must first go to a Bible school. All these things are good, but the Lord can also use you when you have none of these opportunities.

19

Hi, Brother!

Let me tell you about a prisoner I met some years ago in Bermuda. I had spoken to a big group in the prison, and a black guard asked me, "Will you go with me to some cells where there are people who really need your advice?" I went into that part of the prison where the men were kept who were not even allowed to attend meetings.

I saw two men in a cell. One of them had a round, red rag on his back.

"Has that man tried to run away?" I asked the guard.

"Yes," he replied. "How do you know that?"

"Because of the red tag on the back of his uniform. I have been in three prisons, and we were also forced to wear red tags on our uniforms, if we tried to run away."

"This man is a murderer, and he was sentenced to whippings. He was so afraid of the whippings that he tried to run away. Poor fellow, he has had a double portion."

When I saw him sitting there on the floor, the expression on his face reminded me of a wounded animal, and my heart went out to him. I prayed, "Lord, help me to find a way to his heart." I went to him with my Bible in my hand and asked him, "Say, fellow, have you had a whipping?"

"Yes."

"Was it bad?"

"Yes."

"Did they take you to the hospital afterwards?"

"No, it was not that serious."

He stood up and came to the barred door, probably thinking to himself, "That woman is sure asking me strange questions!"

Then I asked, "Did they treat your wounds?"

"Yes, they did. They rubbed them."

"Is there hatred in your heart?"

"Hatred? My whole heart and my whole life are full of hatred."

"I can understand that."

"Ha! You?"

Then I told him how I had felt when they whipped my sister, because she was too frail and weak to shovel sand. How hatred had come into my heart!

But I said, "Fellow, a miracle happened then. Jesus brought into my heart God's love through the Holy Spirit, and I had no hatred. I could forgive.

"And when you receive Jesus Christ as your Saviour, He will fill your heart—not with hatred but with love. How do you do it? You just come to Him and say, 'Lord Jesus, will You be my Saviour?' The Lord is willing to be that. Then you must ask Him to come into your heart. And He *will* come, because it is written in the Bible, and the Bible is true. Jesus said:

> Behold, I stand at the door, and knock: if any man hear my voice, and open the door, I will come in to him . . . .
>
> Revelation 3:20

"Fellow, when the Lord Jesus comes into your heart, there is love in your heart. The worst may happen in your life, but the best remains."

I prayed with that man, and then he prayed. I believe I had never heard such a strange prayer. The man had never prayed before, but one of the things he did was thank Jesus that He had died for him on the cross.

Have you ever thanked Jesus for that?

I shook hands with the man. Then he said, "Have you another five minutes?"

"Sure. Why?"

"On the other side of the corridor, in the third cell, is a man in great darkness. Please, tell him also of Jesus."

I went to the man in the third cell. I told him about Jesus, and how I prayed for him! When you speak about Jesus, you can always pray at the same time. You can have the vertical and the horizontal connection at the same moment.

The man in the third cell said his *yes* to Jesus. I mean a real *yes*—a decision.

I had to leave the prison then, but I first passed the cell of the murderer. "Say, fellow, that was good that you sent me to the third cell. He also has accepted Jesus Christ as his Saviour and Lord."

The man looked around me and shouted across the corridor, "Hi, brother!" A babe in Christ, a few minutes old, and he already had a burden for souls. How old are you?

When someone becomes a Christian he becomes a brand new person inside. He is not the same any more. A new life has begun! All these new things are from God who brought us back to himself through what Christ Jesus did. And God has given us the privilege of urging everyone to come into his favor and be reconciled to him. For God was in Christ, restoring the world to himself, no longer counting men's sins against them but blotting them out. This is the wonderful message he has given us to tell others. We are Christ's ambassadors. God is using us to speak to you: we beg you, as though Christ himself were here pleading with you, recieve the love he offers you—be reconciled to God.

2 Corinthians 5:17–20 LB

20

Corrie's Message

In New Zealand I visited a small prison, where there were probably no more than fourteen men. We had a good time together. The men were sitting with their backs against a wall, and I was sitting in front of them, speaking about the great joy of knowing that you are a child of God.

I told them that when you ask Jesus to come into your heart and you confess your sins, then He does a great miracle in your heart, which He Himself calls "being born into the family of God." At that time you may say to God, "Father, my Father." And He says to you, "My child."

Four of these men made a decision. Each wanted to give his heart to Jesus, to be cleansed and born into the Kingdom of God—to be born a child of God.

Before I left, I shook hands with all the men. One was a very old man. He cried and held my hand and kissed it. I was a little bit amused about that, and finally said, "Now, friend, let me go, and the Lord bless you." Then he let go of my hand.

This man was sentenced to a long imprisonment for the crime of manslaughter. The woman with whom he lived had snored one night when he was drunk. He strangled her because of her noise. When he realized that the woman was dead, he was so scared he ran straight to the police and told them, "I have murdered my wife."

"Why are you crying so?" I asked him.

He replied, "Because I am so happy. I have always had such terrible feelings of guilt because I killed the woman I lived with. Now I have brought it to the Lord Jesus, and I know I am forgiven. I am a child of God! Jesus is in my heart."

A year later I went back to that prison, and I talked with some of the men there. I asked where the old man was, and they told me, "He died some time ago."

One of the men took me aside and said, "I must tell you something. Whenever that man heard me going through the corridor, he called me into his cell. He would say, 'Let us talk about Corrie's message.'"

How happy I was that the Lord had used me to help that man!

21

Conversations in Prisons

I know there are almost insurmountable problems when you are in prison. I would like to write about some of the problems we discussed when I talked with prisoners in America.

Ann

"What is the most difficult thing that you have to go through?" I asked Ann.

I sat with her in her cell in solitary confinement. She showed me a photograph of her husband and children. "Because of my crime, I have given them such a hard life. They lack a wife and mother and they have to bear the shame—all because of the bad things I have done."

She told me that she had accepted Jesus as her Saviour ten years ago, but had solidly backslid. She knew much about the Bible, so it was easy to talk with her.

"There is an answer to your problem, Ann. It is Jesus. He has told us that we may pray for one another. You can pray for your children and your husband. You can tell the Lord everything. He understands you better than any human being.

"I read in the Book of Revelation that not one of our

prayers is lost. They are kept in heaven. That is how important they are in our heavenly Father's eyes.

"You feel guilty that your family has to suffer because of you. You carry that guilt. I have a book here. It must lie somewhere: on my hand, on the table, or on the floor. It is the same with your guilt. It must lie somewhere. It is lying on you. You are carrying it.

"Now the Bible teaches us a mystery. When Jesus died on the cross, God laid on Him the guilt of the whole world. Jesus was willing to bear that terrible death, to carry our sins, our guilt. You may bring your sins, your guilt to Jesus, and He will forgive you and make you clean. Then He will fill you with the Holy Spirit. The fruit of the Spirit is peace and joy and love. Then you will be able to think of your husband and children with peace."

Ann said, "I believe all you tell me, but I cannot accept it now. I have been away from the Lord for so long. Ten years ago I could have accepted it, but now it is too late."

"Ann, do you remember the story of the lost sheep? A shepherd had one hundred sheep. One evening when he came home, he saw that one sheep was lost. What did he do?

"He left the ninety-nine at home and went to look for that one lost sheep. He found it, took it on his shoulder, and brought it home.

"You are a lost sheep. Jesus will bring you home. The shepherd rejoiced and organized a feast to celebrate the finding of the lost sheep. Jesus rejoices when He finds you. Only tell Him everything. He loves you. Confess your sins to Him and ask Him to come into your heart. He will rejoice, and you will rejoice."

Ann did it. And I know Jesus rejoiced!

Frank

"Trust and study the Bible, Frank. It is the Word of God. You have asked Jesus to come into your life, and He came. Now all the promises of the Bible are yours."

Frank had seen one of Billy Graham's meetings on television and he had joined the many who came to Jesus that evening.

"Do you know what my problem is when I read the Bible?" Frank said. "It all happened so very long ago. I have seen Christians who were really happy, but after a while they backslid. Their Christianity did not last long."

"Frank, what can help you and give you solid ground to stand on is your faith in Jesus. He is the same yesterday, today, and tomorrow. He never changes. He is the same now as He was in Israel two thousand years ago. He is a solid rock to stand upon.

> On Christ the solid rock, I stand.
> All other ground is sinking sand.

"Talk much with Him. He is here *now*. He loves and understands you."

Roger

He was a young man in a big prison. I had spoken in the chapel, and while he cleaned the table where we had had some refreshments, I had an opportunity to talk with him.

Without looking up, he said, "I am afraid."

"Who are you afraid of? The guards?"

"No, the men around me. They say that they will kill me if I do not do what they ask me to do. They tell me to do dirty things, which I cannot refuse."

"Roger, I was in a prison where the devil was strong, and I was afraid, like you are. I saw then that I was weak, and the devil was stronger, much stronger than I. But then I saw Jesus, who is much stronger than the devil. Jesus and I together could overcome the devil. When I realized that, miracles happened.

"Paul, in the Bible, had a problem in his life. The Bible

does not tell us exactly what it was, but he calls it a 'thorn in the flesh, messenger of Satan, to harass me.'

"You can read about it in Second Corinthians 12:7–10. Paul asked God to take it away, but God did not remove that thing. He answered Paul, 'My grace is sufficient for you, for my power is made perfect in weakness.' God does not always remove difficult things from our lives, but His grace in us *is* sufficient to overcome the difficulties."

> Have you got any rivers you think are uncrossable?
> Got any mountains you can't tunnel through?
> God specializes in things called impossible.
> He can do what no other can do.

22

Mike

"I am going on parole next week."

"Boy, that is good! Are you glad?"

"No, this was my fourth time in prison, and soon it will be my fifth. I know myself."

"No, Mike, Jesus has found you, you have found Jesus, and you and He together will overcome the temptations. Read the story of Gideon in Judges six.

"Gideon was neither strong nor courageous. He hid himself in a barn, in the bottom of a winepress. But how did God see him? The angel who came to him said, 'The Lord is with you, you mighty man of valor.' Because the Lord was with him, Gideon changed from a weakling into a strong overcomer. The Lord said to him, 'Go in this your strength.'

"Mike, the devil is stronger—much stronger than you and me—but Jesus is much stronger than the devil, and with Jesus, we are stronger than the devil.

"It is important that you do what Jude said, 'Stay always within the boundaries where God's love can reach and bless you' (Jude 21 LB).

"If, when you leave prison, you go straight to a bar and get yourself drunk and renew your relationship with the friends who helped you to go to prison through their advice and assistance in your crimes, you can be sure that you will find yourself in this building for the fifth time. You stand on victory ground with Jesus, but you must be willing to go the whole way with Him. You are free to choose."

"That is exactly my problem. I am willing now to be a good guy, but what happens when I am free?"

"Mike, you are not the only one who has this problem, but the Lord knows that. The Bible supplies the answer when it says, 'Be filled with the Spirit' in Ephesians 5:18. A Spirit-filled Christian is a difficult target for the enemy, for he has the fruit of the spirit and the gifts of the Holy Spirit, which are like a good armor and weapons in his hand. A compromise with the enemy is deadly dangerous, just as if a soldier on the front line helps the enemy to attack him and his fellow soldiers.

"If, again and again, you lay your weak hand in the strong hand of Jesus, you will be able to remain within the boundaries where God's love can reach and bless you."

"How do you do that? It all sounds so nice when you say it, but how do I lay my hand in Jesus' hand?"

"Get used to telling Jesus everything. He understands you and loves you. You might say to Him, 'Jesus, I need money badly. I can make a lot of money quickly if I go to that bar and plan a little job with one of my friends. I can also get something to drink there, and I really want a drink. Jesus. Take my hand, fill me with Your Holy Spirit. Keep me from falling!'

"If you say that, Jesus will help you. He is not only willing, but also able to help you. Ask Him to help you find people who love Him and who are willing to show you how to understand the Bible. Fellowship is so important. Read the Bible much. When you find a text that helps you more than others, write it down, and put it in your pocket, and learn it by heart.

"Mike, the most important thing is *trust Jesus*. He will help your faith to grow. In Hebrews twelve He is called the author and finisher of your faith. I like helping you very much, and pray that the Lord will give me wisdom on advising you. Jesus likes to help you even more, and He *really* is able to help."

23

Joe

"I heard your talk today about how to become a child of God by Jesus Christ. It made me anxious to do it. But, lady, you do not know what kind of a guy I am. I have murdered people, and don't ask me how! Let's be honest—I am a lousy guy. No, I am not made of the wood from which you can cut and shape a Christian."

"Joe, there are two ways that we know our sins. The devil accuses us night and day. I don't know if you know the devil. I know him. He speaks very clearly, and he says, 'What you have done is what you are, and what you will always be. There is no hope for you.'

"The devil is a liar! The Bible tells us something different. When you bring your sins to Jesus, when you confess your sins, He is faithful and just to forgive you, and He will cleanse you with His blood. You don't understand that? It does not matter. He does it, and it works!

"The Bible also promises that He will put your sins as far away from you as the east is from the west. It is as though He has cast them into the depths of the sea—forgiven and forgotten."

I met Joe again a month later. He looked quite different. The first thing he said was, "I have done it! I was totally miserable! They put me in the hole, which I had feared they would do. I had been in there before for a very long time.

"On my first day in it again, I figured I had nothing to lose and I said, 'God, if You do exist, take this miserable life of mine in Your hand.' At that very moment something happened. It was as if I was no longer alone. I can't tell you exactly how it was, but I felt happier than ever before. Was it the Lord who came to me? I could suddenly talk to Him. I remembered everything you had said and I asked myself, 'Is what she said true?'

"I slept better that night than I had for weeks, and when I woke up, I felt that happy feeling again. I must say that the weeks I spent in that hole were happy. I knew I was not alone, and to my amazement, I was taken out of the hole after only two weeks.

"Now, Miss ten Boom, I believe it all! How good it is to read the Bible. You had told me that Jesus knocks at the door of your heart, and so I said, 'Come in.' I have told Him more than anyone else all that I have done wrong and through that, I believe there was a clearing up of the dirty mess."

"Joe, you can read in John three what took place in your life. In that chapter Jesus tells about what happens when you accept Him. You were born again. Now God is your Father, Joe, and what a Friend you have in Jesus! I'm so glad that the Bible is not fantasy. It is not imagination, not feelings, not philosophy—it is reality! The greatest reality is that Jesus is here on this earth right now, through His Holy Spirit. You are here. I am here. Jesus is here, too."

24

So Long!

When you believe the Lord Jesus Christ and you ask Him to come into your heart and into your life, He gives you *His* freedom and a new dimension of living that circumstances cannot destroy.

We can all get to heaven
Without health—
Without wealth—
Without fame—
Without learning—
Without culture—
Without beauty—
Without friends—
Without ten thousands of things.
But we can never get to heaven without Christ.

God promises us forgiveness for what we have done, but we need His deliverance from what we *are*. He conquered death at the cross and He went to heaven. He pleads for us there.

At the same time He is in heaven, He is also with us! I do not understand it at all, but I know it works. I have experienced His presence in the deepest hell that man can create. I have really tested the promises of the Bible, and believe me, you can count on them.

I know that Jesus Christ can live in us—in you and me—through His Holy Spirit. We can talk with Him. We can tell Him everything. You can talk with Him out loud or in your heart—when you are alone, as I was alone in solitary confinement, or in a place crowded with people. The joy is that He hears each word!

In Ravensbruck, after a terrible winter, it was decided that all prisoners my age and older should be killed. One week before this was to happen, I was set free. Later, I learned that it was done only because of a clerical error. In recording our numbers, my number had mistakenly been transferred from the death column to freedom!

A blunder of man, yes. But I knew it was God's way of telling me that I must share—for the rest of my life—what I had learned about Him.

That is why I wanted to write this book for you. I am eighty-five years old now, and I know that the moment is coming when I will have to die. But I am not afraid of death. I belong to Jesus. All of my tomorrows are in His hands.

You know, eternal life does not start when you go to heaven. It starts the moment you reach out to Jesus. That is where it *all* begins. He never turned His back on anyone, and He is waiting for *you!* God bless you.

Appendix of Helpful Scriptures

The Bible is a source of strength and wisdom. Read the Word of God often. I have written down some texts which have helped me. I pray that the Lord will bless these texts and this book for *you*.

Feeling Alone

Be strong and of good courage, do not fear or be in dread of them: for it is the Lord your God who goes with you; he will not fail you or forsake you.

Deuteronomy 31:6 RSV

"Come to me, all who labor and are heavy laden, and I will give you rest. Take my yoke upon you, and learn from me; for I am gentle and lowly in heart, and you will find rest for your souls. For my yoke is easy, and my burden is light."

Matthew 11:28–30 RSV

"... I give them eternal life, and they shall never perish, and no one shall snatch them out of my hand. My Father, who has given them to me, is greater than all, and no one is able to snatch them out of the Father's hand."

John 10:28, 29 RSV

"If a man loves me, he will keep my word, and my Father will love him, and we will come to him and make our home with him."

John 14:23 RSV

[Jesus said,] ". . . I will never fail you nor forsake you." Hence we can confidently say,

> "The Lord is my helper,
> I will not be afraid;
> what can man do to me?"

Hebrews 13:5, 6 RSV

Temptation

No temptation has overtaken you that is not common to man. God is faithful, and he will not let you be tempted beyond your strength, but with the temptation will also provide the way of escape, that you may be able to endure it.

1 Corinthians 10:13 RSV

Do you want more and more of God's kindness and peace? Then learn to know him better and better. For as you know him better, he will give you, through his great power, everything you need for living a truly good life: he even shares his own glory and his own goodness with us! And by that same mighty power he has given us all the other rich and wonderful blessings he promised; for instance, the promise to save us from the lust and rottenness all around us, and to give us his own character. . . . Then you must learn to know God better and discover what he wants you to do. Next, learn to put aside your own desires so that you will become patient and godly, gladly letting God have his way with you. This will make possible the next step, which is for you to enjoy other people and to like them, and finally you will grow to love them deeply. The more you go on in this way, the more you will grow strong spiritually and become fruitful and useful to our Lord Jesus Christ.

2 Peter 1:2–8 LB

Stay always within the boundaries where God's love can reach and bless you. Wait patiently for the eternal life that our Lord Jesus Christ in his mercy is going to give you. Try to help those who argue against you. Be merciful to those who doubt. Save some by snatching them as from the very flames of hell itself. And as for others, help them to find the Lord by being kind to them, but be careful that you yourselves aren't pulled along into their sins. Hate every trace of their sin while being merciful to them as sinners.

Jude 21–23 LB

How can a young man stay pure? By reading your Word and following its rules. . . . I have thought much about your words, and stored them in my heart so that they would hold me back from sin.

Psalms 119:9, 11 LB

Worry

"Therefore I tell you, do not be anxious about your life, what you shall eat or what you shall drink, nor about your body, what you shall put on. Is not life more than food, and the body more than clothing? Look at the birds of the air; they neither sow nor reap nor gather into barns, and yet your heavenly Father feeds them. Are you not of more value than they? And which of you by being anxious can add one cubit to his span of life? And why are you anxious about clothing? Consider the lilies of the field, how they grow; they neither toil nor spin; yet I tell you, even Solomon in all his glory was not arrayed like one of these. But if God so clothes the grass of the field, which today is alive and tomorrow is thrown into the oven, will he not much more clothe you, O men of little faith? Therefore do not be anxious, saying, 'What shall we eat?' or 'What shall we drink?' or 'What shall we wear?' For the Gentiles seek all these things; and your heavenly Father knows that you need them all. But seek first his kingdom and his righteousness, and all these things shall be yours as well."

Matthew 6:25–33 RSV

Part Three

Don't Wrestle,
Just Nestle

Foreword

"Baby, just cry. Don't look at the people or mind what they are thinking about you. Just cry." I felt an arm around me, hid my face on her shoulder, and cried. Then I heard her singing softly:

> His eye is on the sparrow,
> And I know He watches me.

Yes, my comforter was Ethel Waters. I had heard her sing those words before, but they had never touched me so. For this time, she was singing that song for me, and I needed her song.

This happened the first time I saw the movie, *The Hiding Place*. In my mind I found myself reliving the suffering of my family. I saw Father and Betsie, both lost in prison. I had to put up with the horrible cruelties again. That was why I cried.

But then my eyes were turned in the right direction by Ethel Waters' song. There *is* One who watches me, and the secret of abundant life is literally "Don't wrestle, just nestle." What a security!

1

Prescription for Anxiety

Why should I feel discouraged, Why should
    the shadows come,
Why should my heart be lonely And long for
    Heav'n and home,
When Jesus is my portion? My constant Friend
    is He:
His eye is on the sparrow. And I know He
    watches me.

"Let not your heart be troubled," His tender
    word I hear,
And resting on His goodness, I lose my doubts
    and fear;
Tho' by the path He leadeth But one step I
    may see:
His eye is on the sparrow, and I know He
    watches me.

Whenever I am tempted, Whenever clouds arise,
When songs give place to sighing, When hope
    within me dies,
I draw the closer to Him, From care He sets me free;

His eye is on the sparrow, and I know He
cares for me.

MRS. C. D. MARTIN

This century has been called the Age of Anxiety. How fitting that description is! Everywhere I go, I find people tormented by inner tensions, nervous strain, worries, and fears. We are a generation of worriers, always taking pills to cure our anxieties and relax our nerves.

There is a great deal of difference between worry and concern, and we must realize this. Concern makes us do something to ease the situation. It moves us to take constructive action. But worry burdens our minds and bodies without helping us to find a solution to the problem. Worry is like racing the engine of an automobile without letting in the clutch. You burn energy, but you don't go anywhere.

No doctor has a cure for worry. Oh, he can give you an aspirin for your headache or something for your nervous stomach. He may even give you one pill for your tensions and another pill for your insomnia. But these are not cures. They just cover up the real problem.

There is a permanent cure for worry. The prescription is not mine—it was given by Jesus almost two thousand years ago, in His Sermon on the Mount. He devoted a great deal of this talk to the problem of anxiety. Therefore, here is His prescription for anxiety.

Remember the Power of God

A few weeks before the Sermon on the Mount, Jesus walked along the shore of the Sea of Galilee and called twelve men to lay down their fishing nets and follow Him. They would be His disciples. The men saw the presence of God in Jesus. They wanted to follow Him, but still, they had questions—many questions.

"If we don't fish for a living, how will we support our families?"

"How can we be fishers of men? We're afraid to talk to other people."

"How can we carry the Gospel to the world? Just the thought of doing that fills us with fear!"

Jesus went up on a mountain to escape the huge crowd that kept following Him. When He was in a private place, He sat down, gathering His disciples around Him. He began to teach them about the Kingdom of God. The disciples, who had followed Jesus for a little while now, knew He had no money of His own. Yet He never worried. He seemed content.

"What is the secret of happiness?" they asked.

Jesus replied:

> ... don't worry about living—wondering what you are going to eat or drink, or what you are going to wear. Surely life is more important than food, and the body more important than the clothes you wear. Look at the birds in the sky. They never sow nor reap nor store away in barns, and yet your Heavenly Father feeds them. Aren't you much more valuable to him than they are? Can any of you, however much he worries, make himself even a few inches taller? And why do you worry about clothes? Consider how the wild flowers grow. They neither work nor weave, but I tell you that even Solomon in all his glory was not arrayed like one of these! Now if God so clothes the flowers of the field, which are alive today and burnt in the stove tomorrow, is he not much more likely to clothe you, you "little-faiths?" So don't worry and don't keep saying, "What shall we eat, what shall we drink or what shall we wear?" That is what pagans are always looking for; your Heavenly Father knows that you need them all. Set your heart first on his kingdom and his goodness, and all these things will come to you as a matter of course. Don't worry at all then about tomorrow. Tomorrow can worry about itself! One day's trouble is enough for one day.
>
> Matthew 6:25–34 PHILLIPS

Actually, Jesus was chiding them a bit, saying "You already have life and a body, and they are far more important than what to eat and wear. Does it not follow that the God who is capable of making a human body is capable of putting clothes on it and providing food to keep it going?"

The next time you find yourself depressed or worried about some big problem, remember the power of God. Remember His great miracle of bringing you into being, and you will know He is more than able to care for you.

I remember reading a story about Bishop Quayle, who must have had a keen sense of humor. He told of a time when he sat up late in his study, worrying over many things. Finally the Lord came to him and said, "Quayle, you go to bed. *I'll* sit up the rest of the night."

A friend of mine told me, "When I worry, I go to the mirror and say to myself, 'This tremendous thing that worries me is beyond solution. It is even too hard for God to handle.' And then I smile."

Remember the Foolishness of Worry

Jesus had a way of asking embarrassing questions. "Which of you by taking thought can add one inch to your height?" Can you worry yourself taller? Or shorter? You might worry yourself dead, but never will you worry yourself happier. That comes by a different method.

Alcoholics Anonymous has sound advice to offer their people—advice all of us could use—in the prayer, "O God, give us serenity to accept what cannot be changed, courage to change what should be changed, and wisdom to distinguish the one from the other."

I like that, for there are two things we should not worry about: the things we can change (we need to get busy and do something about these) and the things we cannot change (no amount of worry will help these). Instead, we should let God give us the courage and strength to master the unavoidable, for with God, nothing is impossible.

"Don't be fools; be wise: make the most of every opportunity you have for doing good. Don't act thoughtlessly, but try to find out and do whatever the Lord wants you to do" (Ephesians 5:16, 17).

Jesus says that God is concerned about us personally. "Look at the birds of the air," Jesus said to His disciples. "God feeds them in spite of the fact they cannot drive a tractor, plough a field, or work a harvesting machine. They can't even build barns to store the grain. Yet God takes care of each one of them." Then He turned to His disciples, and I imagine He had a slight smile on His face. "Are you not of more value than they?"

Next Jesus pointed to the wild flowers that were poking their heads around the rocks in the hard soil of Israel. "Look at them," He said. "They can't run a spindle or loom, they don't even have the ability to sit down at a sewing machine and make their own clothes. But see how beautifully God has dressed them. Why? Because God cares for even the grass of the field." Then He said, "If God so clothes the grass of the field, will he not much more clothe you?" (*See* Matthew 6:25–30.)

Count Your Blessings

I was in Japan, very tired, with a stomach that was upset from the unusual food. How I longed for a good European meal, a table where I would not have to sit cross-legged on the floor, and a soft bed instead of the hard mats the Japanese sleep on. I was filled with self-pity. I wanted to be back in Holland!

That night in church, while I was busy feeling sorry for myself, I saw a man in a wheelchair. After the service my interpreter took me down to meet the man, a bent little fellow with yellow skin and slender hands. His face wore the happiest expression I could imagine.

"What are those little packets on your lap?" I asked the

man, pointing to several packages wrapped in brown paper and tied with string.

He broke into a wide grin and tenderly unwrapped one of the packages. It was a sheath of pages covered with Braille, the raised script of the blind. "This is the Gospel of John, written in Braille. I have just finished it," he said.

Then he continued. "This is the fifteenth time I have written the Gospel of John in Braille. I have also written other of the Gospels, as well as many shorter portions of the Bible."

"How did you come to do this?"

"Do you know about the Bible women here in Japan?" he asked. "Bible women go from village to village, bringing copies of the Bible, books, and literature to those who are hungry for God. Our Bible woman is very ill with tuberculosis, but she travels every week to sixteen villages, even though she will soon die. When I heard about it, I asked the Lord what I could do to help her.

"Although my legs are paralyzed, and I cannot get out of the wheelchair, in many ways I am healthier than she. God showed me that though her hands are shaky and my legs paralyzed, I could be the hands, and she the legs. I punch out the pages of Braille, and she takes the Bible around to the villages and gives them to the blind people, who miss so much because they cannot see."

I left the church that night filled not with self-pity, but with shame. Here was I, with two good legs for traveling all over the world, two good lungs, and two good eyes, complaining because I didn't like the food!

These precious people had discovered a sure cure for self-pity—service to others. Perhaps it is like the slogan I once saw on a church sign in America. "If you are unhappy with your lot in life, build a service station on it." The best antidote I know for self-pity is to help someone else who is worse off than you.

"I complained that I had no shoes, then I saw a man who had no legs, and I stopped complaining."

Walk With God

Does the Lord Jesus say, "Come along now. Take it easy. Don't worry," leaving us to realize that there have never been so many reasons to worry as there are now?

No! The Lord gives an answer.

"Seek first his kingdom and his righteousness" (*see* Matthew 6:33 KJV). It is your relationship with your heavenly Father that is important. That is what determines whether you will be victorious or defeated, however difficult the circumstances are.

The day after He fed the 5,000, Jesus chastised the crowd that followed Him, accusing them of following Him because He had fed them. "But you shouldn't be so concerned about perishable things like food. No, spend your energy seeking the eternal life that I, the Messiah, can give you. For God the Father has sent me for this very purpose" (John 6:27).

Still the crowd was more concerned with food. They asked Him to give them free bread every day, as Moses did in the desert. Jesus told them, "Moses didn't give it to them. My Father did. And now he offers you true Bread from heaven. The true Bread is a Person—the one sent by God from heaven, and he gives life to the world" (John 6:32, 33).

The crowd, still not understanding what Jesus was telling them, asked that they might have every day the bread He was describing.

"I am the Bread of Life. No one coming to me will ever be hungry again. Those believing in me will never thirst," Jesus told them (John 6:35). Although He said this over and over again to the crowd, they still failed to understand or accept. Many of His disciples left Him at this point. Jesus then turned and asked the twelve if they, too, were leaving Him.

Simon Peter answered for all of them: "Master, to whom shall we go? You alone have the words that give eternal life, and we believe them and know you are the holy Son of God" (John 6:68, 69). Peter and the others who stayed with Jesus knew what was important and what was not. They knew the way to victory.

With your hand in the Father's hand, you stand on victory ground. Give room for the Holy Spirit. He gives you the right outlook on troubling events. I know that from the time that I saw my sister Betsie starving in a prison camp. We were surrounded by people who had behind them a training in cruelties, but we had moments when we were conscious that we were walking with the Lord.

Often we had to go too early to roll call, which started at 3:30 A.M. Betsie and I would walk through the camp, and there were three of us present. Betsie said something, I said something, and the Lord said something. I can't tell you how, but both Betsie and I understood clearly what He said. These walks were a bit of heaven in the midst of hell. Everything around us was black and dark, but in us there was a light that belonged to eternity.

Jesus said:

> All who listen to my instructions and follow them are wise, like a man who builds his house on solid rock. Though the rain comes in torrents, and the floods rise and the storm winds beat against his house, it won't collapse, for it is built on rock.
>
> Matthew 7:24, 25

From My Notebook

Today is yesterday's tomorrow you worried about, and all is well.

If God sends us on stony paths, He provides strong shoes.

Faith is blind—except upward. It is blind to impossibilities, and deaf to doubt. It listens only to God and sees only His power and acts accordingly.

S. D. GORDON

Jesus is always victorious. We only have to get into the right relationship with Him and we shall see His power being demonstrated in our hearts and lives and service. And His victorious life will fill us and overflow through us to others. That is revival in its essence.

ROY HESSION

Worry is the interest you pay on trouble before it comes.

God will not tolerate anything in our life that takes the supreme place which is His by right.

Jesus Christ can transform our . . .

fear into faith
anxiety into adoration
worry into worship.

2

No Time for Anxiety

... Our fears for today, our worries about tomorrow, or where we are—high above the sky, or in the deepest ocean—nothing will ever be able to separate us from the love of God demonstrated by our Lord Jesus Christ when he died for us.

Romans 8:38, 39

We were in Africa. Prisoners were dancing. The pounding rhythm created an atmosphere of demonical darkness. The expressions of the dancers' faces made me afraid. It was as though they were dancing themselves into a trance, possessed by dark powers. Their shouting influenced the other dancers, causing the gloomy darkness in their eyes to increase every minute.

These people were criminals. They knew what it was to be inspired by hell itself. Next to me were three black Christian brothers, who had accompanied me to this place hidden far away in the jungle—the place where I was to speak. We waited for the prison director to join us.

At last he came. He was a friendly man, but I could see that he knew how to make people obey. "I am so glad you came to speak to my men." He clapped his hands and shouted, "Stop dancing! Sit down and listen to what Miss ten Boom has to tell you."

I saw the anger flash in their eyes. It was hard for these men to part from the spirits who had kept them in their power. About four hundred men settled down in front of me, and about two hundred were standing behind me. I saw not one friendly face among the six hundred: I looked at my three black Christian brothers and felt uneasy that not one white man had accompanied me. I underestimated those men badly, as I later clearly discovered.

I softly prayed, "Lord, I know that those who are with me are more and stronger than those who are against me. Let Your never-failing love fill my heart and mouth, and also the man who will interpret for me."

I spoke rather a long time to those prisoners, and I saw the expressions on their faces change as they heard me say, "Jesus loved *you* when He died on the cross for the sins of the whole world." I never saw such a dramatic change in people. They came from darkness into light; from the darkness of hell into the light of heaven.

As we waited at the gate while a guard found the key, a prisoner came running toward me. He took my hand and said something. My interpreter translated, "You came to us because God's love is in you. Thank you. Thank Him!"

We squeezed into the tiny car and headed down the primitive path through the jungle, going toward Kampala. The moment we got into the car, my three brothers began to sing and praise the Lord. I was sitting in the front seat, squeezed against the driver. The other two men were crowded into the tiny backseat. But even our cramped positions did not keep them from singing and praising God as we roared through the dense jungle.

What a strange sight we must have been, bouncing down the jungle road, weaving from side to side to miss the holes and puddles, singing and praising the Lord in loud voices!

I saw a man ahead, standing on the side of the narrow road. He had the tire and wheel from a car leaning against his leg.

The driver slowed the car to a stop and shouted across me, "What is the matter, my friend?"

"Please bring me to Kampala," he pleaded. "My tire is flat, and my wheel is broken."

What a pity we have no room, I thought.

But my happy black brothers saw no such problem. "Of course," they shouted together. "Join us. We like to help our brothers in the name of Jesus."

The man came around to the other side of the car, to get into the front seat between the driver and me. While he was walking around, one of the men in the backseat leaned forward and whispered. "Pray with us, Tante Corrie, that we bring him to the Lord before we reach Kampala."

How they squeezed him in, I'll never know. But soon we were on our way again, the man jammed between the driver and me holding that big, rusty car wheel and the dirty black tire on his lap. The men in the car began singing and praising the Lord again, keeping time with the bumps in the road.

The driver began to talk to the man in his own language, and the other men enthusiastically entered in. I could not understand what they were saying, but I knew they were talking to him about the Lord Jesus. I prayed, keeping my eyes on the road.

Suddenly the passenger looked at the driver and said something. One of the men in the backseat interpreted for me. The passenger was asking if he knew the driver. Hadn't they met before?

"Sure," the driver answered. "Last year you and I were in the same prison, where we have just been with Miss ten Boom. You know, boy, at that time I served the devil. Now I serve Jesus Christ. He uses me to save lives of other sinners, and He will use you from now on, also."

The man with the big wheel on his lap listened intently. Before long, he accepted Jesus as his Saviour. I wanted to join in the men's happy praises, but I was too concerned about the road and the wild way in which the driver was swerving from side to side. *Surely we'll all be killed,* I worried.

Then, ahead, we saw a woman with two children waiting alongside the road. "Let us give her a lift and also bring her to Jesus," one of the men shouted.

Did he really mean it? There was absolutely no room!

The car stopped, and for a minute I entertained the hope that they were just going to witness to her where she was and drive on. But no, they motioned her to join us in the car!

As she got in the backseat with her two children, I saw a third child come out from under her coat. Somehow they all got in, sitting on top of one another. One of the small children had to crawl over my shoulder and sit on my lap. I could not feel my legs. Never, never had I been in such an overcrowded automobile—and on such a terrible road.

We started up again, the car rolling from right to left, left to right, bouncing off rocks and logs alongside the road, weaving over shaky jungle bridges. But the black men were tremendously happy, believing the Lord had put the woman there so they could pick her up and witness to her. This time, all four of the men—including the one with the big wheel on his lap—eagerly joined in the conversation, telling the woman about the Lord Jesus Christ.

Suddenly the four men began to sing. *"Tuku tenderesa Jesu,"* an African song of praise. The woman had accepted Jesus as her Saviour and Lord.

We arrived in Kampala and swerved through the traffic, the men still singing and banging their hands against the side of the automobile in time with the music. Our fellow travelers left us—the man with the big wheel and the woman with her three children—but not until my friends had obtained their names so they could follow up their work. Then they took me to the place I was staying.

After they had gone, I sat for a long time, rubbing life back into my legs and trying to get some insight into the events of

the afternoon. While I, the cautious European, had been so
anxious and worried about the fierce prison, the horrible
road, the old car, and the discomforts and dangers of the trip,
my black brothers had no time for anxiety. They were too
busy praising God and sharing the good news with those
whom God sent into their path. They did not see the people
along the road as problems, but as opportunities.

Perhaps, I thought, as I lay back on the bed to rest my aching body, if I would spend less time worrying whether the car
would run, the road was paved, or the bridges would hold—
and lose myself in praise and service as these African brothers
did—I would not only live longer, but more abundantly.
While I was anxious about reaching my destination, they
were excited about meeting people along the way. Reaching
the destination seemed almost incidental to praising God and
serving Him as they went.

Maybe the way in which we travel and the attitude we
have while making our way through life is more important
than reaching our destination. Or could it be that in God's
sight, the way actually *is* the destination?

Jesus said ". . . I am the Way—yes, and the Truth and the
Life . . ." (John 14:6).

From My Notebook

It is better to burn out than to smolder out without having warmed one heart for the Lord Jesus.

Happiness is not dependent on happenings, but on the relationship that persists in the happening.

When we act on the Word of God, and not on our feelings, we experience that God means His promises. The fact is that God watches over His Word to perform it.

> Slow me down, Lord,
> I am going too fast,
> I can't see my brother,
> When he is going past.
>
> I miss a lot of good things
> Day by day,
> I can't see a blessing
> When it comes my way.

When the heart has learned to trust Him as He should be trusted, utterly without reservations, then the Lord throws wide the doors of the treasure house of grace. He bids us go in with boldness and receive our share of the inheritance of the saints.

Be sure you remain covered with a canopy of praise. It is

like a tent over and around you. Satan has no entrance as long as you pin down the sides by praising, and thank God for His wonderful promises.

In the life of the true believer there are no accidents.

My little children, I am telling you this so that you will stay away from sin. But if you sin, there is someone to plead for you before the Father. His name is Jesus Christ . . . .

1 John 2:1

3

Worry

Don't worry over anything whatever; whenever you pray tell God every detail of your needs in thankful prayer, and the peace of God, which surpasses human understanding, will keep constant guard over your hearts and minds as they rest in Christ Jesus.

Philippians 4:6 PHILLIPS

Before the battle, the general always sends his spies into the enemy camp. They take photographs of secret defenses, they learn the enemy's battle positions, their ammunition supply points, even the personal weaknesses of the opposing leaders. But unless the general passes this information on to his own troops, they cannot win the battle.

That is why I want to share with you some of the things I have learned about the enemy and about the Victor, Jesus. I want you to know that God expects us to be conquerors over the powers of darkness—not only for the sake of our personal victory and for the liberation of others who are in bondage to Satan, but for His glory. He wants the world to know that He is triumphant and victorious, and the only way it will ever know is by our demonstration of God's power and authority.

Once a man saved up his money for years and bought the house of his dreams. It was in the countryside, with mountains and streams all around it. He could not wait to begin living in his new house, but because of his business, he could not move in for several months. So he allowed the man who was living there to stay as a caretaker until he was ready to move in himself.

But when the new owner came to move into his dream house, the other man said, "No, I am staying here. You find somewhere else to live."

"But you promised you would move out when I was ready," the owner said.

The man gave a laugh and replied, "This is my home. You cannot come in." Then he slammed the door in the owner's face and locked it.

The owner marched straight to the police station with his papers of ownership. The next time he knocked on the door of his house, there were two large policemen standing next to him. When the man in the house saw the policemen, he meekly packed his belongings and left the house to its owner.

What the true owner of the house could not do in his own strength, he was able to do when he appeared with authority on his side. It is the same with us. Satan may laugh at us and continue to afflict us with disease, fear, anxiety, and defeat. But when we come to him in the name of Jesus, he knows we have all the authority of the Kingdom of God behind us, and he must flee.

Worry Is Sin

I had to learn that worry is sin before I could get rid of the worry. First I tried to "fear not" as an act of obedience. It was as successful as trying to kill a lion with a toy gun. Then I began to learn the secrets. First you must ask forgiveness for your sin of worry. Then you need to accept the cleansing of the blood of Jesus. Finally, you need to let God fill you with the Holy Spirit. When you are filled with the Holy Spirit, the spirit of fear will flee, forced out by power and love and a sound mind.

In the latter part of 1946, a group of Christian ladies in Ottawa asked me to give my testimony at an evening meeting.

I did not even know where I would sleep that night, but I went in obedience. I felt it was a training in trusting God. How good that the coach was the Lord Himself!

It was the first time that I had been in Canada. I remember that the spirit of worry was very busy with me. Sometimes my traveling went smoothly. God gave me friends who organized my meetings, and I went where He told me to go. But now I was not quite sure of the Lord's guidance. At such moments I felt far from Holland. A big ocean was between my hometown and me.

So often that tramp for the Lord, the prisoner Paul, had helped me. I opened my Bible and read what he wrote from his prison in Rome: "Be careful for nothing; but in every thing by prayer and supplication with thanksgiving let your requests be made known unto God. And the peace of God, which passeth all understanding, shall keep your hearts and minds through Christ Jesus" (Philippians 4:6, 7 KJV).

My, but Paul knew about worry! Still, he found the answer: "I can do all things through Christ which strengtheneth me" (Philippians 4:13 KJV).

I did not even know where I would sleep that night, but God had used Paul to encourage me, and I trusted Him.

That evening, I told my problem to the dear people who heard my talk, and sure enough, a lady came to me and said, "You are very welcome in my home. I have a small guest room you may use." I had been worried about finding a place to sleep, but the Lord had the answer all worked out for me!

What a joy to be surrounded by kind people. Before I fell asleep, I thought of the time shortly before, when enemies were all around me, and how they hated me because of what I had done for the Jews. Soon I was sound asleep.

Suddenly the light in my room came on. I opened my eyes, and a uniformed officer was standing in front of me. My only thought was, *This is the Gestapo. They have found me.* I said to the man, "I am not a Jew." Then I remembered where I was and told him that I was a guest of the lady of the house. Without a word, the man put the light out and left.

What had happened? He was the owner of the house and had come home late. He did not want his wife to see him at that hour, especially since he had been drinking too much that night. He decided to go to the guest room, but his plan misfired because of my presence there. When he told his wife, she was very disturbed. What a shock it must have been for her guest! She put on her robe and ran to my room. There she found me, fast asleep!

Some months later, I met my host again. It was a bitterly cold evening. I had spoken that afternoon in a town some distance from Ottawa, where I was to speak in the evening. Friends had brought me to a house halfway between the two towns, and my former host was waiting there. He told me that he was going to take me to Ottawa, where the meeting was to start at 8 P.M.

The highway was so icy that we skidded from right to left. I looked at my friend and saw that he had given himself courage for the drive by taking some drinks, and it was not a little amount that he had enjoyed. I thought about the coming evening. How could I sit for hours in that car, worrying about the slippery road and his driving, and then still have the power to speak? I couldn't. I was worried—I thought I had reason to be—but I knew that my worry was a sin. I would have to ask forgiveness for my sin and trust the Lord to deliver us safely to Ottawa.

I prayed for strength and then said to the driver, "Jim, I am going to speak tonight, and it is impossible for me to worry for several hours beforehand, while you skid from right to left and left to right. So I hope you don't mind, but I am going to sleep."

Jim smiled and said, "You go ahead. I will drive and not sleep." And he did. The Lord gave me a very good rest.

The young girl who was my secretary at that time was sit-

ting behind me, and she told me later that I snored all the
way. That was a comfort to her, because she knew that I was
not worried, but she said it was still the most terrible car ride
of her life. We arrived safely, on time for the evening meeting, and I was refreshed and ready for my talk.

God's Armor

The battle always has to be fought before the victory is
won, though many people think they must have the victory
before the battle. The conflict with worry and fear is almost
always there—each person must overcome or be overcome.
But we must fight each battle of our lives in the strength of
Jesus' victory. He said, "As the Father has sent me, even so I
am sending you" (John 20:21). We are to be like Jesus—One
of whom Satan is afraid!

When we worry, we are carrying tomorrow's load with
today's strength; carrying two days in one. We are moving
into tomorrow ahead of time. There is just one day in the cal-
endar of action—today. The Holy Spirit does not give a clear
blueprint of our whole lives, but only of the moments, one by
one.

We all have the same enemies—we are all preyed upon by
frustration and worry. In India, Australia, Japan, Germany—
we need the same Holy Spirit. We need to remember that we
are children of God, living within His constant care. God
knows and is interested both in the hardest problems we face
and the tiniest details that concern us. He knows how to put
everything in place, like a jigsaw puzzle, to make a beautiful
picture.

But Satan has a very good secret service. The moment you
step out from under God's umbrella of grace, you are discovered and attacked by Satan. Recognition of Satan's attack is
half the fight. An attacking enemy who is not recognized already has half his battle won. Never knowing where, how,
and when Satan will attack us, we should never be unpro-

tected or unprepared. We need to be clothed with the whole armor of God.

> Last of all I want to remind you that your strength must come from the Lord's mighty power within you. Put on all of God's armor so that you will be able to stand safe against all strategies and tricks of Satan. . . . So use every piece of God's armor to resist the enemy whenever he attacks, and when it is all over, you will still be standing up.
>
> Ephesians 6:10, 11, 13 LB

What a relief to know that we do not need to provide the armor! God makes the armor—we just put it on. But the armor has no protection for the back, for God does not expect any deserters. Neither is the armor a museum piece—it is given for us on the battlefield. Jesus is Victor!

Every temptation to worry or fear is an opportunity for victory. It is a signal to fly the flag of our Victor. It is the chance to make the tempter know anew that he is defeated.

> Thine, O Lord, is the greatness, and the power, and the glory, and the victory, and the majesty: for all that is in the heaven and in the earth is thine; thine is the kingdom, O Lord, and thou art exalted as head above all. Both riches and honour come of thee, and thou reignest over all; and in thine hand is power and might; and in thine hand it is to make great, and to give strength unto all.
>
> 1 Chronicles 29:11, 12 KJV

From My Notebook

Worry is a cycle of inefficient thoughts, whirling around a center of fear.

Worry is often carrying a load that one should not carry at all.

Worry is distress of mind, not concern. Some people ought to have *more* concern.

It is sinking under the sense of responsibility, yielding to the fear that there may be failure, instead of gripping the lines and whip and determining to ride down the chance of its coming.

S. D. GORDON

God gives us His power to bear all the sorrow of His making. But He does not give us the power to bear the sorrows of our own making, which the anticipation of sorrow most assuredly is.

IAN MACLAREN

The purpose of being guilty is to bring us to Jesus. Once we are there, then its purpose is finished. If we continue to make ourselves guilty—to blame ourselves—then that is sin in itself.

4

May a Christian Worry?

Why, therefore should we do ourselves this wrong,
Or others—that we are not always strong,
That we are ever overborne with care,
That we should ever weak and heartless be,
Anxious or troubled, when with us is prayer,
And joy and strength and courage are with Thee.

AUTHOR UNKNOWN

We imagine that a little anxiety and worry are indications of how wise we are. We think we see the dangers of life clearly. In reality, however, our fears are only an indication of how wicked we really are.

As Charles G. Trumbull says:

Worry is sin; a black, murderous, God-defying, Christ-rejecting sin; worry about anything, at any time whatever. We will never know victory over worry and anxiety until we begin to treat it as sin. For such it is. It is a deep-seated distrust of the Father, who assures us again and again that even the falling sparrow is in His tender care.

The words *fear not* occur many times in the Bible. The Word of God has no suggestions; only commandments. So if we fear and worry, we are being disobedient, and disobedience is always a sin.

The only way blunders and destruction can occur in our lives is when we forget to trust God. When we take things into our own unskilled hands, we get everything knotted and tangled.

Worry is utterly useless. It never serves a good purpose. It brings no good results. One cannot think or see clearly when worrying. Let pagans worry, if they will, but we must not, for we have a living Saviour, our Lord Jesus Christ, and His conquering power. His victory can be our victory. Life at best is brief, and there is so much to be accomplished. If we must burn ourselves out, let us burn out for God.

In this age of increasing pace, it is so easy to follow the crowd and let materialism become our god. But if we do, only too often we find that worry and tension become our masters. The effects of tension are seen in all spheres of life. Tension leads to inefficiency and frayed nerves with our fellow workers and students. In politics, it leads to strain in international relations and fears of war. In the home, tension leads to irritability with our husband or wife, destroying the very thing God meant to be perfect.

For with people who are not content, worry has a fair chance. Paul writes:

" I have learned to be content, whatever the circumstances may be. I know now how to live when things are difficult and I know how to live when things are prosperous. In general and in particular I have learned the secret of facing either plenty or poverty. I am ready for anything through the strength of the One who lives within me" (Philippians 4:11–13 PHILLIPS).

Lonely Contentment

I have never been so poor as the time that I was in solitary confinement. How difficult it was to learn to be content. But Paul wrote once, while in prison, that we are God's workmanship. I experienced the same. The lessons were difficult, but the Teacher was so powerful. The Lord was my all-sufficiency. I wrote home: "The Lord Jesus is everything to me. He never leaves me alone. I concentrate on the Saviour. With Him there is certainty, with the other things, only uncertainty and delayed hope, which hurts the heart. Once I asked to be freed, but the Lord said, 'My grace is sufficient for you.' "

That brought my thoughts to Paul. *He* had to learn a lesson. Three times he asked the Lord to take away the thorn in the flesh (*see* 2 Corinthians 12:8). Then he got this answer: God's grace was sufficient for him. That was true for Paul and it was true for me. In a way I knew that there was a danger that the joy I felt and my security in Him would lose some of their power when I was free; when the securities of the world would once again be a comfortable foundation to rest upon.

When the Lord gives you the ability, through His grace, to accept the situation, that contentment can help you to get rid of your worry, whatever happens. But could I ever accept being a prisoner alone in a cell? I surely could not, but Paul told about all grace, always, in all things (*see* Corinthians 9:8).

Once when I was in the cell, I heard the bolt on the outside of my door being undone. A guard opened the door and commanded, "Follow me!" I was being called out to be questioned. It was the first time I had left the cell during that lonely imprisonment. Yes, lonely—night and day I was alone. First we had to go through long corridors with cell doors on both sides, then through a door which opened onto the outside. I breathed deeply. I was in a courtyard. The walk was almost too short to the small barracks where people were questioned. I looked up to the sky, then around me, and then down and saw blades of grass and some tiny white flowers. The little flower "Shepherd's purse" was growing between the bricks used to pave the courtyard.

When the guard who accompanied me looked the other way, I quickly bent down and picked some of those little flowers and hid them inside my dress. When back in my cell, I took a broken medicine bottle, arranged my bouquet, and put it behind my cup so that the guards could not see it when they looked through the peephole in my door. That tiny bouquet was my garden, and I enjoyed it as the only nice thing in my cell.

I was ready to accept my little bouquet of six blades of grass and three little flowers as my garden because of Him who was in me, and I could say then with Paul, ". . . I look upon everything as loss compared with the overwhelming gain of knowing Christ Jesus my Lord. For his sake I did in fact suffer the loss of everything, but I considered it mere garbage compared with being able to win Christ" (Philippians 3:8 PHILLIPS).

Demon Influence

When we are worrying, we are not trusting. Yet we who have burdens and responsibilities are inclined to worry. Again, it is so important that we recognize the enemy. Worry and depression are sister and brother. I want to tell you about something that I experienced—a time when the influence of depression was practically nationwide.

After I was released from the German concentration camp, I returned to Holland until the war was over. Then God told me to go back to Germany, to carry the good news of Christ's victory over fear and guilt. When I arrived in Germany, however, I found the people in great confusion. Many German people had beloved relatives missing. Were they still in Russian concentration camps? Had they died in battle or in the horrible bombings? This uncertainty drove many people to desperation.

Many of these people were turning to the fortune-tellers to find their answers. While the evil spirits, working through the fortune-tellers, often gave just enough accurate information to keep the people coming back, something else also happened. Many of those who visited the fortune-tellers later developed horrible fears, depression, and anxiety. Their hearts, it seemed, were always in the gloom of darkness. They often had the urge to commit suicide. I immediately recognized this as sure evidence of demon influence.

Jesus said, "I am the Light of the world. So if you follow me, you won't be stumbling through the darkness, for living light will flood your path" (John 8:12). Even if a child of God has visited a fortune-teller and come under demon influence, he does not have to remain in darkness. He can be set free.

Realizing this, I began speaking against the sins of the occult. It was the occult that was putting people in bondage, causing them to break down mentally and spiritually. I often read Deuteronomy 18:10–13 to point out how these sins are an abomination in the sight of God. Instead of depending on God's power, the people were rushing to the enemy for help. And as we know, the enemy is a liar, whose very purpose is to deceive people and lead them away from the truth.

I showed the German Christians how Jesus Christ has provided an answer to this serious problem. Satan is not the Victor, Jesus is. And even if the people had invited the demons in, Christ could overcome that. They did not have to live with their depression or fear any more. They had to be set free. I was able to say to them:

> . . . [God] gave you a share in the very life of Christ, for he forgave all your sins, and blotted out the charges proved against you, the list of his commandments which you had not obeyed. He took this list of sins and destroyed it by nailing it to Christ's cross. In this way God took away Satan's power to accuse you of sin, and God openly displayed to the whole world Christ's triumph at the cross where your sins were all taken away.
>
> Colossians 2:13–15

In the Old Testament there is an interesting story of the lost axhead. A son of the prophets had been chopping wood, and his axhead had fallen into the Jordan River. Since it was a borrowed ax, he was worried and afraid. He ran to Elisha for help. Elisha sent him back to the place where he had made his mistake, so the miracle of restoration could happen. The axhead floated to the surface, the young man grabbed it and replaced it on the handle (*see* 2 Kings 6:1–6).

Just so, you need to go back to the place where you opened the door of your life to the influence of the spirit of worry. Where did the fear enter? What was it that caused you to start worrying? Remember, the spirit of fear does not come from God. Instead, God gives us power and love and a sound mind (*see* 2 Timothy 1:7). Therefore, you need to ask the Lord Jesus to close the door that you opened.

How is this done? First you need to recognize that you have sinned. Most fear, anxiety, and worry come through the sin of not trusting God.

Second, confession is necessary. Face yourself. Tell God. And then, if possible, confess to someone close to you. When all of this is done, you may then claim the precious promises for cleansing. You will instantly be freed from the bondage of Satan.

Worry is a demon—fear of demons comes from demons themselves. As children of God, we have nothing to fear. He who is with us is much stronger than he who is against us. "And he asked them, 'Why were you so fearful? Don't you even yet have confidence in me?' " (Mark 4:40.)

"The seed among the thorns represents those who listen and believe God's words but whose faith afterwards is choked out by worry and riches and the responsibilities and pleasures of life . . . " (Luke 8:14).

May we worry? We have a whole Bible as our guide, Jesus Christ as our living Saviour who loves us, and heaven as our future!

From My Notebook

Worry is an old man with bended head,
Carrying a load of feathers which he thinks are lead.

Worry means two enemies—the thing you worry about and the worry!

Why don't we try something lighter than worry? Worrying people are like tightrope walkers going over a rope from the past to the future. They balance between hope and fear. In one hand they carry a sack with the undigested past, in the other hand a sack with the anticipated future.

The heart lays aside its fears amid the accumulated blessings of our heavenly Father. Worries pass away like cloudlets in the warmth of a summer's morning.

> Yesterday He helped me,
> Today He did the same.
> How long will this continue?
> Forever, praise His name.

5

Fear

For God hath not given us the spirit of fear; but of power, and of love, and of a sound mind.

2 Timothy 1:7 KJV

Fear is the atmosphere of worry. Nothing weakens us as much as fear. On the other hand, nothing weakens the tempter as much as a quiet, bold, steady fearlessness. Satan cannot operate in the atmosphere of trust.

Oh, but fear and worry can talk so wisely! You may often think they are right, but fear is often a stupid blunder. Once I worked for a month in Los Angeles during a flu epidemic. One morning my secretary woke up with a bad headache, and I feared that she had the flu.

"Girl, please stay in bed. I have to go to a college to speak at nine o'clock, but I will go alone," I told her. Once I was outside, I felt a headache myself. My eyes felt so strange. I knew that headaches and eye problems were sometimes symptoms of the flu, and I worried all the way to the college. I had so much work to do—I didn't have time for the flu!

Once at the college, I opened my Bible to begin my talk and found that I could not read even one letter! Fear whispered, "You have the flu in your eyes." I was not sure that was possible, but I listened to my fear. What would I do if I could not read? I need to prepare for my talks and to study the Bible, if I am to speak about the Lord. Could I go back to my former trade of watchmaking? Impossible! I would need my eyes more for that than for any other trade.

I know that I did not give a happy talk that morning, for when worry and fear are on the throne, you are not an open channel for streams of living water. It is impossible to listen to the Lord's voice while listening to your own fear. Fear is so loud, so insistent, so time-consuming!

Near the end of my talk, my secretary came quietly into the room and sat down in the back row of the auditorium. When I finished my talk and the students left, I went to her. "Why didn't you stay in bed, when you had such a headache?"

"Oh, I am not ill. My headache is gone," she answered.

"All right, but it could have been the beginning of the flu. You should have stayed home and started answering the letters that I gave you."

"That's why I came. I couldn't work, because you have *my* glasses!" Both our glasses had exactly the same frame, but far different lenses! We both laughed at our mistake. My flu had gone. So had my headache. Once we traded glasses, I could read perfectly, and I was ashamed to have listened to my silly, blundering fear all morning.

Trust the Vine

Anxiety, fear, and worry are the result of our unwillingness to trust God. To worry is the same as saying to God, "I don't believe You." Do you fear for your finances? Are you afraid you won't be able to feed or shelter your loved ones? Do you lie awake and fear your fears? Listen to what God says!

"Give your burdens to the Lord. He will carry them. He will not permit the godly to slip or fall" (Psalms 55:22).

"And it is he [God] who will supply all your needs from his

riches in glory, because of what Christ Jesus has done for us" (Philippians 4:19).

"Stay away from the love of money, be satisfied with what you have. For God has said, 'I will never, *never* fail you nor forsake you.' That is why we can say without any doubt or fear, 'The Lord is my Helper and I am not afraid of anything that mere man can do to me' " (Hebrews 13:5, 6).

Remember when Jesus told the parable of the vine and the branches in John 15? He said the secret to abundant living is in staying attached to the vine. An unattached branch has something to fear. Not only can it not produce fruit, but it will be burned in the fire. But an attached branch has no fears. All it has to do is nestle close to the vine, and the vine does all the work, sending its sap through the branch and producing luscious grapes. It is not the branch that produces the grapes, it is the vine.

"But if you stay in me and obey my commands, you may ask any request you like, and it will be granted! My true disciples produce bountiful harvests. This brings great glory to my Father" (John 15:7, 8).

Fear does not take away the grief of yesterday, nor does it solve the problems of tomorrow. All it does is rob you of the power of today. Rather than wind up on a psychiatrist's couch or an undertaker's slab, do what God tells you. Seek first His Kingdom and His righteousness. He will add everything else you need.

Fear or Victory?

There are many people who don't realize that fear is the enemy. When the fight is on and blows are being exchanged, fear is a sure element of defeat. Fear sucks the spirit out of one's fighting, takes the nerve out of one's courage, robs vim and zest from one's action. But this is always a false fear, because it tells us the enemy is stronger than we are. That is not true! We know that Jesus is Victor, and a fear that tells us otherwise is false.

When you become a child of God, you are a target for the enemy, and he will do his utmost to tell you that you are crazy. Sometimes you think that you are not a Christian when you have trouble, but I should very much doubt whether you are a Christian at all if you did *not* have trouble.

The whole of the New Testament and the history of the Church shows that when we are children of God, we are in a fight of faith. Not having any troubles in your life is therefore far from being a good sign. It is indeed a serious sign that there is something radically wrong. There is a special reason for my saying that, because we are special objects of the attention of the enemy. Why not have problems when it is God's way to bless you!

"... count it all joy when ye fall into divers temptations" (James 1:2 KJV). That is the way your faith is proved. The devil cannot rob us of our salvation, thank God! But he can make us miserable. He can fill us with his false fear.

It is the tempter who knows real fear. His fear is founded on fact and experience. He has met One greater and stronger than himself. Satan is afraid of his Victor. He knows what it means to be thwarted and resisted, beaten back steadily and driven clear off the battleground. There has been a man upon the earth whom Satan fears—whom he can neither trust nor resist—Jesus Christ. He learned to fear Him in Nazareth and in the wilderness. Jesus' absolute, steady obedience to the Father beat Satan. Even the storm on Galilee's blue waters, so unusually violent that it frightened the experienced sailors, failed to touch Jesus with fear.

Fear is as common as sin. If we could be wholly free of fear, we would have stronger bodies, minds, spirits, faith, courage, and power. The tempter continually plays on our sense of fear. For instance, people's fear of being in personal want is holding back huge amounts of money—money which could change the condition of the whole heathen world and move forward the date of Jesus' coming.

At our side there is always conflict with the tempter. Each of us must overcome or be overcome. Our victory comes through Jesus' victory, and we must fight in the strength of His victory. Throw out your self-seeking spirit—it allows Satan a free hand to do as he chooses. Yield to the Holy Spirit. He will burn out your self-spirit.

Men as Trees Walking

In his book *Spiritual Depression, Its Causes and Cure,* Dr. D. Martyn Lloyd-Jones wrote about the great importance of living as rich as we are in Jesus Christ.

> If all Christians simply began to function as the New Testament would have us do, there would be no problem of evangelism. It is because we are failing as Christian people in our daily lives and witness that the Church counts for so little and so few are attracted to God. So for that most urgent reason alone, it behooves us to deal with this question.

We are like the man who was blind and healed, but still saw men as trees walking (*see* Mark 8:22–26). Yes, we have received the healing touch from Jesus—we were born again the moment we asked Him to come into our hearts—but people around us are not envious to receive the same. This is simply because we do not behave like happy, fearless people. We have unlimited riches through the promises of the Bible and the presence of the Lord in our hearts, but we still see men as trees walking.

Jesus asked the blind man, "Can you see?"

The man answered, "Not quite one hundred percent, Lord." How good it was that he told the Lord! Jesus gave him another touch of healing, and his eyesight was perfect. I am sure that even if Jesus had not asked him, the man would have told the Lord the problem and been satisfied.

So, if your sight is still only partial, tell the Lord, "Thank You, Lord, for what You did, for what You gave me—but I need more."

For Jesus said, "Blessed are they which do hunger and thirst after righteousness: for they shall be filled" (Matthew 5:6 KJV). He did not tell the blind man, "Try hard to see." The man had only to ask, and it was given to him.

You and I must ask Jesus to do the job through His Holy Spirit. He is the One who makes our eyes to see. "But when the Holy Spirit controls our lives he will produce this kind of fruit in us: love, joy, peace, patience, kindness, goodness, faithfulness, gentleness and self-control . . . " (Galatians 5:22, 23).

We are often too content with a partial healing. I had an experience of liberation from resentment some time ago. Some friends, fine Christian people, had done something really mean against me, and I had forgiven them. That is what I thought.

A friend asked me how the situation was, but I told him, "I don't want to talk about it. I have forgiven it."

"I understand that," he answered, "but I should like to know what they think about it."

"Oh, they take it easy. They simply say that they have never done it. Perhaps they forget that I have everything in black and white, in the letters which they wrote to me at that time."

My friend looked at me and waited a moment. Then he said: "Where are *your* sins? You told us in your talk this morning that when we confess our sins, God casts them into the depths of the sea and you even believe that there is a sign saying No Fishing Allowed. But the sins of your friends you have in black and white. 'Lord, I pray that You will give Corrie the grace to burn all the black and white of the sins of others today as a sweet-smelling sacrifice before she goes to bed.' "

I surely did, and how well I slept that night. Now when I

meet these people, I enjoy a peace that makes our friendship an unusual joy.

No, it was not easy. As a matter of fact, I needed the Lord just as much as when I had to forgive the people who had been cruel to my family. Forgiving is a hard job. But in 2 Corinthians 9:8 Paul tells us that there is always grace, sufficient for everything. The Holy Spirit taught me a prayer that always helps me, "Thank You, Lord Jesus, that You brought into my heart God's love through the Holy Spirit. Thank You, Father, that Your love in me is stronger than my resentment" (*see* Romans 5:5).

No compromise. The Lord is willing and able to give us clear sight. When worry gets static, it becomes depression. When unforgiveness is healed, there is a liberation that makes the enemy run.

Have you the black and white of the sins of others? Burn them today. Together with the Lord, you can.

Children of the Light

One time, artists were invited to paint a picture of peace. The pictures were many and varied, but the winner depicted a little bird sitting calmly on her nest, which was built on a slender branch overhanging Niagara Falls. The peace of the little bird did not depend on her surroundings. And so it is with us. As Christians, our peace of heart and freedom from fear do not depend on our circumstances, but on our trust in God. Fear is want of faith.

Being a Christian does not mean there is no more battle. It means we have a strategic point of attack in the battle. The battle position of the Christian is victory, joy, and abundance. The Lord expects us to do no more than welcome His assistance. The doors of heaven are open. If I hold on to feelings that prevent me from living under an open heaven, then it is no wonder I am fearful and depressed.

A great note of joy and victory is sounded in the book of

Philippians—a book, incidentally, written from prison. Here
Paul says:

> Don't worry about anything; instead, pray about everything; tell
> God your needs and don't forget to thank him for his answers. If
> you do this you will experience God's peace, which is far more
> wonderful than the human mind can understand. His peace will
> keep your thoughts and your hearts quiet and at rest as you trust
> in Christ Jesus.
>
> Philippians 4:6, 7

It is God's intention that we live as children of the light.
He wants us to be strong, free, peaceful, and happy. This was
the secret Nehemiah learned when he was tempted to come
down from the wall he was building around the city of Jeru-
salem. On every side there were worries and fears, but he
grasped God's truth and sang, "The joy of the Lord is my
strength" (*see* Nehemiah 8:10).

Now I have a very practical tip for you. Take good notice
of all the blessings He gives and all those He has given in your
past. As the old hymn says, "Count your many blessings,
count them one by one, and it will surprise you, what the
Lord has done."

> Faith came singing into my room,
> And other guests took flight.
> Grief, anxiety, fear and gloom,
> Sped out into the night.
>
> I wondered that such peace could be,
> But Faith said gently, "Don't you see,
> That they can never live with me?"
> **ELIZABETH CHENEY**

From My Notebook

There is an aggressiveness of love that is fearless. Fear is cowardly. Faith is aggressive, like love and goodness are aggressive. Satan is aggressive in evil, but Jesus is more aggressive in love.

Jesus Christ knows no fear, and He expects you to fear nothing while He is with you. When we confess His lordship and our hearts fully agree, then we turn our lives over into His care. That is the end of worry and fear and the beginning of faith.

Worry is double-parking on the avenue of anxiety.

$$- \text{Christ} = + \text{fear}$$
$$+ \text{Christ} = - \text{fear}$$

Courage is fear that has said its prayers.

The folly of being anxious about the near future is just as stupid as worrying about what will happen about a thousand years hence. We have to live in the present moment, because we can do nothing about the past, and God is doing everything about the future.

GEORGE MACDONALD

God has made me put my heel on the neck of worry, of weakness, of fear, of inability, and I stand and declare that whosoever believes in Jesus shall not be put to shame.

E. W. KENYON

6

Frustration

Even if we have learned how to deal with anxiety, worry, and fear, the enemy has yet another powerful weapon he uses on us—frustration. Frustration is dangerous because it is so simple to blame it on others, to think there is nothing *we* can do to overcome the problem. And yet even the most frustrating of circumstances can be turned to good, if we use the opportunities we have.

I find it a great frustration to have a message but have no one to give it to. On one trip to Russia I had such a frustrating time! I wanted to tell everybody, especially the communists, about the Lord Jesus Christ. However, whenever I tried to talk to people on the streets of Moscow, I found they would always be looking over their shoulders. Finally they would rush away, afraid someone would see them talking to the old woman with a Bible. I became so frustrated, anxious, and filled with despair. I was in Russia, but I could find no one who would listen!

One afternoon I met a young woman, and we chatted about ordinary things—the weather, the tulips in Holland, the price of gasoline. I sensed she was hungry to hear more about the Lord, but I knew she was afraid to talk in the park. I invited her to come to my hotel room for a good talk.

"Oh, no," she whispered, glancing every which way. "The tourist hotel rooms here are the most dangerous places to talk. There is a hidden microphone in each room. Every word you speak is put on a tape and played before the officials." She excused herself and moved quickly away from me.

The next morning my companion and I were sitting in our hotel room, totally defeated. We had been in Russia one week and had not been able to speak to a single communist about the Lord Jesus.

Suddenly I spotted something on the floor, just under the edge of the bed. It was a pattern of tiny holes, like those in the top of a pepper shaker. Suddenly I had a tremendous inspiration. "Thank You, Lord," I said to myself. "That surely must be the place where the microphone is hidden." Reaching for my Bible, I bent low over the holes in the floor and began to speak in a deliberate voice.

"You who listen have many problems, just like every other human being. Two of these problems are common to all men—sin and death. I have here in my hand a book. It almost bursts with good news. In this book—it is called a Bible—you can read everything you need to know about the answers to these problems. The answer is found in the life of a man, the Son of God, Jesus Christ. He died on the cross for the sins of the whole world, and for your sins also. He carried the punishment you and I deserve. But not only did He die for us, He rose from the dead and is alive today. Yes, He is even willing to live in you through His Holy Spirit. If you will accept Him, He will give you the power to overcome death also and live forever with God in heaven."

For almost five minutes I preached into the hidden microphone, knowing that my sermon was not only being heard, but was being recorded on a tape recorder and passed on to superiors. What a joy! I finished my sermon by saying, "Jesus said once, 'Come unto me, all you who labor and are heavy laden, and I will give you rest.' Since all men in Russia know the meaning of labor, then it means that Jesus must love Russians in a special way. When He says 'all,' He is talking to all who listen to this tape."

From that day on, I gave the microphone a little sermon every morning, bringing a simple Gospel message and hope to my unseen hearers.

After leaving Moscow, we traveled to Leningrad, where once again I discovered the pepper-shaker holes in the floor. That night I gave a five-minute sermon to my hidden listeners. The next morning, two serious men came in and took a seat at the table next to ours at breakfast. From their appearance and the way they dressed, I was sure they were members of the secret police.

For a moment I was disturbed and frustrated. Then I saw what God was doing. My microphone sermon had brought results! Instead of being worried, I should rejoice. This was simply another opportunity to present the Gospel.

I asked my companion, in English, "Do you know that you can become a child of God?"

She immediately grasped what I was doing and began to play her role. "I can never be a child of God," she said, shaking her head. "I am not good enough."

"Ah ha," I answered. "That is exactly what I expected you to say! But you see, only sinners are eligible." As we talked I kept noticing the two men at the next table. They tried to pretend they were not interested. One man had a newspaper in front of his face. But I could see they were leaning in our direction, trying to hear every word.

We continued our conversation, speaking as loudly as we could without making it obvious. We stayed at it until we were satisfied these men could never say they had not heard the Gospel. We even repeated the whole conversation in German, in case they couldn't understand my English!

Do you think I was playing a silly game, talking into hidden microphones and giving my testimony at breakfast? It was no game at all! After one whole week of frustration, I was at last giving my message to the communists. Not in the way

I would have preferred, it is true. But who can say that those few men who heard me were not important to the Lord? Even when we are denied a big opportunity, we must make the best of all the little ones that come our way.

I remember a story about the little boy and his sister. They were trying to climb a steep mountain. The little girl began to complain, "Why did God put all these rocks here?"

Her brother reached back and patted her on the shoulder. "These are really stepping stones," he said. "God put them here to help us reach the top."

Many people are worried and frustrated because they never have the opportunity to do what they want to do. I have found the seeming obstacles are really opportunities within themselves. If we do what our hand finds to do, then God will open up broader places of service.

Many years ago I heard of an old Dutchman and his young son. They had to walk home at night across the *polders,* the dried sea bottom where the water had been pumped out and held back by dikes. The little boy was afraid, for he knew there were still deep pockets of water and many patches of quicksand on the polders. All they had to give them light on the walk was a small kerosene lantern.

"Please, Father," the boy begged, "don't make me walk out there. It is so dark, and the lamp only gives light enough for one step at a time."

The father took his son's hand in his own. "That's right, but one step at a time is all the light we need. And if we walk in the light we have, we have enough light for the next step. However, if we stand still, waiting for enough light to see the entire way home, then even the light we have will burn out, and we will be left in the dark."

And so they made their way home safely, one step at a time, walking in the light. Every obstacle, every frustration, can become an opportunity if we trust God and walk in the light we have.

From My Notebook

You are on the road to success if you realize that failure is only a detour.

In order to realize the worth of the anchor, we need to feel the stress of the storm.

When a train goes through a tunnel and it gets dark, you don't throw away your ticket and jump off. You sit still and trust the engineer.

Our trust and hope are not in the promises, but in the One who made the promises.

Our faith may falter, but His faithfulness, never!

We are to do heavenly business. The earthly part of it is only a detail.

> Some wish to live within the sound
> Of church and chapel bell
> I want to run a rescue shop
> Within a yard of hell.
>
> C. T. STUDD

We will see more and more that we are chosen not because of our ability but because of His power that will be demonstrated in our not being able.

What can you and I pray for leaders? Pray for the Christian leader that God will guide him. Pray for the non-Christian leader that God will control him.

Faith sees the invisible, believes the unbelievable, and receives the impossible.

Luther said, "Work as though He will not be coming for a thousand years. Be ready as if He should come today."

Men have to go through many experiences in order to get the spiritual vision which is needed to see the divine plan. A film is always developed in a dark room.

7

Don't Burden Yourself

Let him have all your worries and cares, for he is always thinking about you and watching everything that concerns you.
1 Peter 5:7

Many years ago, shortly after World War II had come to a
close, I was invited to speak in a Japanese church in Tokyo.
The nation was still reeling from the impact of the war. All
that the Japanese people had believed in had been snatched
away, and two of their greatest cities had been destroyed by
the atomic bomb. If ever a people had reason to worry, it was
the Japanese.

Because of the language barrier, it seemed practical for me
to give them an object lesson. "Do you know the feeling," I
began, "when your heart is like a suitcase with a heavy
load?"

The sad-faced people in the little church all nodded. They
knew the feeling.

I picked up my suitcase and put it on the table. It was very
heavy. I told them how weary I was from tramping all over
the world, carrying that suitcase filled with heavy objects.

"My heart was like that until just last week, when I read a
glorious verse in the Bible. It says, 'Cast all your anxieties on
him, for he cares about you.' I did that. I brought all my bur-

dens to the Lord—all my cares—and I cast them upon Him."
I opened my suitcase and spread it out on the table to demonstrate. "Lord," I continued, "here are my co-workers. They are so tired." I reached down and took two items out of the suitcase and laid them on the table.

"And here is my trip, Lord—the one I have to make next week to the town where I don't know a single person. You know how worried I am about that, and how afraid I get when I think about it. I cast this care on You, too, Lord." I took a big package out of the suitcase and laid it on the table next to the two smaller packages.

"Here are my friends at home, Lord. They wrote about a car accident. Will You please heal them?" I took out one more object and placed it on the table.

"And here is that boy who refused to give his life to Jesus. Dear Lord, You know how much I have worried about him." I placed a heavy piece on the table.

"This is my unbelief. Almost always when our hearts are heavy, it is because we have an unconfessed sin. Forgive me, Lord, and cleanse me with Your blood. Holy Spirit, give me faith and trust."

I took object after object out of the suitcase, mentioning each one as a particular burden or worry. "This is my pride. This is my self-seeking. . . ." In the end, the suitcase was empty, and I said, "Amen!" I closed the empty suitcase and pretended to walk out of the room, swinging my light bag as though it was made of paper.

The people immediately got my point, and the light of understanding broke on their faces. I could tell by their smiles and polite bows when I was finished that the Holy Spirit had spoken truth to them.

After the meeting I quickly threw all the items back into the suitcase and dashed off with my host, to go to the home of the wonderful Japanese Christians who entertained me until it was time to fly on to Hong Kong.

Many years passed, and then I found myself in Berlin, at an international congress on evangelism. After one of the morning seminars, a distinguished-looking Japanese evangelist approached me. "Corrie ten Boom," he said with a broad smile, "every time I hear your name, I think of your trouble suitcase."

"Oh," I said, flattered, "I am so glad you remembered what I said that night."

"It was not what you said that I remember," he smiled courteously, "it is what you did."

"You remember me taking all those objects out of my suitcase and laying them on the table as an illustration of how to pray?"

"No, that is not what I remember most," he said. "What I remember most is that after you finished your talk, you took all the objects, put them back in your suitcase, and walked out of the hall just as burdened as when you came in."

Oh, what a vivid object lesson! That afternoon, back in my hotel room, I began to take a good look at myself. Was I guilty of doing that in my life? How easy it is to unpack my trouble suitcase each morning and cast all my cares on the Father, because He cares for me. But then, as the day goes on, I keep coming back and picking up first this care and then that one, slipping them back into my suitcase. By the end of the day, I am just as burdened as I was at the beginning, and far more exhausted, for I have had to keep slipping back to pick up the cares originally given to my Father.

What about you? Did you unpack your trouble suitcase this morning? Good! But what did you do afterwards? Is your heart still as burdened and heavy as it was before you prayed? Did you repack your suitcase as soon as you emptied it? If so, perhaps you need to return to the Lord, casting all your cares upon Him—for He cares for you. Tell it to Him. The Holy Spirit will teach you how to pray and leave your burdens with the Lord.

Live One Day at a Time

When Jesus told His disciples, "Therefore do not be anxious about tomorrow, for tomorrow will be anxious for itself," He was saying, "Don't try to carry today's burden *and* tomorrow's burden at the same time."

One evening a man stepped into the kitchen to help his wife with the dishes. As he was working, he thought, "If that poor woman could just look ahead and see the dishes that remain to be washed in the future, towering like a mountain ahead of her, she would give up right now!" Then he laughed. "But she only has to wash tonight's dishes, and she can handle that."

As you may know, I grew up in a clock shop. My father was a watchmaker, and I was the first woman in Holland to be licensed as a watchmaker. Our home, the Beje, was filled with the sound of ticking clocks. I still remember the old Dutch parable about the clock that had a nervous breakdown.

The little clock had just been finished by the maker, who put it on a shelf in the storeroom. Two older clocks were busy ticking away the noisy seconds next to the young clock.

"Well," said one of the clocks to the newcomer, "so you have started out in life. I am sorry for you. If you'll just think ahead and see how many ticks it takes to tick through one year, you will never make it. It would have been better had the maker never wound you up and set your pendulum swinging."

"Dear me," said the new clock. "I never thought about how many ticks I have to tick in a year."

"Well, you'd better think about it," the old clock said.

So the new clock began to count up the ticks. "Each second requires 2 ticks, which means 120 ticks per minute," he calculated. "That's 7,200 ticks per hour; 172,800 ticks per day; 1,209,600 ticks per week for 52 weeks, which makes a total of 62,899,200 ticks per year. Horrors!" The clock immediately had a nervous breakdown and stopped ticking.

The clock on the other side, who had kept silent during the conversation, now spoke up. "You silly thing! Why do you listen to such words? That old grandfather clock has been unhappy for years. Nobody will buy him, and he just sits around the shop gathering dust. Since he is so unhappy, he tries to make everyone else unhappy, too."

"But," the new clock gasped, "he's right. I've got to tick almost sixty-three million ticks in a year. And they told me I might have to stay on the job for more than one hundred years. Do you know how many ticks that is? That's six billion, two hundred million ticks. I'll never make it!"

"How many ticks do you have to tick at a time?" the wise old clock asked.

"Why, only one, I guess," the new clock answered.

"There, now. That's not so hard, is it? Try it along with me. Tick, tock, tick, tock. See how easy it is? Just one tick at a time."

A light of understanding formed on the face of the clock, and he said, "I believe I can do it. Here I go." He began ticking again.

"One more thing," the wise old clock said. "Don't ever think about the next tick until you have your last tick ticked."

I understand that was seventy-five years ago, and the clock is still ticking perfectly, one tick at a time.

No man sinks under the burden of the day. It is only when yesterday's guilt is added to tomorrow's anxiety that our legs buckle and our backs break. It is delightfully easy to live one day at a time!

From My Notebook

I took a burden to the Lord
To cast and leave it there.
I knelt and told Him of my plight,
And wrestled deep in prayer.

But rising up to go my way
I felt a deep despair,
For as I tried to trudge along,
My burden was still there!

Why didn't You take my burden, Lord?
Oh, won't You take it, please.
Again I asked the Lord for help,
His answering words were these:

My child, I want to help you out
I long to take your load.
I want to bear your burdens too
As you walk along life's road.

But this you must remember,
This one thing you must know . . .
I cannot take your burden
Until you *let it go.*

BETTY CURTI

8

Prayer

Then another angel with a golden censer came and stood at the altar; and a great quantity of incense was given to him to mix with the prayers of God's people, to offer upon the golden altar before the throne. And the perfume of the incense mixed with prayers ascended up to God from the altar where the angel had poured them out.

Revelation 8:3, 4

Sometimes we underestimate the value of our prayers. In the Book of Revelation, we read how precious they are in God's eyes. They are so precious that they are all preserved there.

When I read this text, I understand a little bit of the great value that our prayers have in the eyes of the heavenly Father. Look back on the prayers you have prayed for that person you are worrying about. Not one of those prayers is lost. They are kept in heaven. What a comfort. What an encouragement!

When Do God's Answers Come?

The Bible says that by prayer and supplication with thanksgiving we should let our requests be made known unto God. Have you ever been discouraged about your praying?

Does it seem your prayers are never answered? Much of our anxiety comes as we worry about others. This isn't helped, it seems, if we pray for others and then do not see our prayers answered. However, let me tell you a few stories that I think will give you encouragement to go on, despite seeming failure.

Not very long ago, I had a wonderful experience in my home country of Holland. I was invited to appear on national television, to bring the Easter message. More than six million people heard my message, I was told. But the most wonderful result was hearing from some people I had not heard from in years—people I had prayed for many years ago.

One man wrote to me and said, "Twenty-five years ago I came out of a concentration camp, into the house you opened for ex-prisoners. You brought me the Gospel. I thought I was not ready for it, but you told me you were going to keep on praying, anyway. Last night I saw you on TV, and now I can say with all my heart, 'I have accepted the Lord.' " It took twenty-five years, but God answered my prayer for that man's salvation!

Another man telephoned. "Forty-five years ago, you told me exactly the same thing you said tonight on TV—that Jesus was the Son of God and is still alive. I always refused to accept Jesus as my personal Saviour. Now I am ready to say yes to Him. May I come to see you?"

Of course I replied, "Please come."

We talked and prayed together. "Now," I said, "ask Jesus to come into your heart."

He prayed, "Jesus, I cannot open my heart. Please, won't You force the door?" And Jesus did a miracle in the life of that man—an answer to my prayer after forty-five years.

When I was fifteen years of age, I spent some time at a secular domestic-science school. Most of the teachers and students did not want me to talk about the Lord. Therefore I spent time praying for them. Following the TV broadcast, I received a letter saying, "Sixty years ago we were together at the domestic-science school. I suddenly remembered that you often talked about the Lord Jesus when we were together. I saw and heard you on TV. I just want to write and tell you that I am a follower of Jesus Christ." Another answer to prayer—sixty years after.

But the most amazing answer came the week after the TV broadcast. When I was five years old, I accepted the Lord Jesus as my Saviour. After that I developed a burden for the people in my town. We lived in Haarlem, quite near the Smedestraat. In this street there were many pubs. Because of the pubs, I often saw many drunken people, some of whom were dragged into the police station on the same street. I wanted so badly to do something to help, but what can a little girl do in such a sad situation? All I could do was pray— and I did a lot of that.

Mother told me later that for a long time every prayer of mine ended with the words, "Lord Jesus, please save those people in the Smedestraat. And save the policemen, too."

Following my TV appearance, I received a letter. "My husband said that it was so nice to hear that you lived in Haarlem. He lived for seventeen years in the Smedestraat, and he worked in the police station in that street. After I heard you on TV, I knew that you would be interested to know that we now know the Lord personally." It took over seventy years for me to hear that my prayer was answered!

Why do I tell you this? To let you know that no matter how discouraged you may be over your prayers, God never lets you down.

Pray Alone and Together

Prayer is the sturdy answer to worry. I urge you to find a place where you can be alone with the Lord. Let it be your own little private prayer chapel.

I understand that Susanna Wesley, mother of Charles Wesley, had her own little private prayer closet. When things got bad in the Wesley household—the children screaming, money scarce, the roof leaking—she would reach down and grab the hem of her long skirt. Separating it from the many long petticoats women wore in those days, she would pull the outer skirt up over her head and close herself in. There she would meet the Lord and commune with Him, returning to her hectic world refreshed and revived.

Prayer should be informal and to the point: conversations with God, so to speak. Nice words do not count. Be definite. If you have a nervous tummy, do not ask the Lord to take it away. Rather, confess where you got it and ask Him to shut the door on the source of your worry.

Pray specific prayers. God does not give stones for bread. If you ask for specific things, you will receive specific answers. Most of us receive not because we ask not, or if we do ask, we ask amiss.

Go to God the same way you would go to your father or mother. Tell Him about your worries. Tell Him you are a sinner because you are anxious and nervous. Be definite. Prayer opens doors to the power that relieves us from anxiety, for God's power is demonstrated in our weakness.

Remember, prayer is not one-way traffic. If it were, it would be similar to someone coming into your house, asking a question, and then leaving without waiting for an answer. Prayer is both asking and receiving, speaking and listening. Yes, that takes time. But you can learn how to converse with God secretly.

But there is more. Not only do we find help for our anxiety by praying alone, but also when we pray with others and have others pray for us. Jesus says He enjoys joining a small group of even two or three who are praying in His name. "... I will be right there among them" (Matthew 18:20). What a marvelous promise! But how many take advantage of it? The best place for group prayer is in the family. Are you a mother? Call the children and ask them to pray with you.

Tell them you are anxious and worried, and ask them to join you in prayer.

The devil smiles when we make plans. He laughs when we get too busy. But he trembles when we pray—especially when we pray together. Remember, though, that it is God who answers, and He always answers in a way that He knows is best for everybody.

From My Notebook

Prayer is the signature of the soul on the correspondence with our Creator.

Prayer changes our attention from the problem to the Power, from anxiety to the Almighty.

Is prayer your steering wheel or your spare tire? Keep on top of your circumstances by keeping the morning watch. Don't allow the circumstances to come on top of you.

> We mutter, we sputter—
> We fume and we spurt.
> We mumble and grumble—
> Our feelings get hurt.
>
> We can't understand things—
> Our vision gets dim,
> When all that we need—
> Is a moment with Him.

To pray only when in peril is to use safety belts only in heavy traffic.

> Fear knocked at the door.
> Faith answered.
> No one was there.

9

God's Answers to Prayer

His love has no limit, His grace has no measure.
  His power no boundary known unto men;
For out of His infinite riches in Jesus,
  He giveth and giveth and giveth again.
                                    ANNIE JOHNSON FLINT

I know many people who trust the Lord for their eternal safety, but they have no faith for the cares of every day. They would find it easy to die, for they know God has promised them a mansion in heaven. In fact, some of them would like to die, just to escape this world. They have no faith for today—just for tomorrow. They do not see that their daily problems are the material from which God builds His miracles.

Once, when I was a little girl, I remember coming to my father with a broken doll. He was busy in the watch shop repairing clocks and watches, but he stopped what he was doing and took special pains to fix my ragged old doll's broken arm. Why did he take this so seriously? Because he saw the doll through the eyes of his little girl. Your heavenly Father loves you. He sees your problems through your eyes. He loves us all and understands our problems. He cares.

When I was in the German concentration camp at Ravensbruck, one bitter winter morning I woke up with a bad cold. My nose was running. Back in Holland I would have been able to adjust to a cold, because I would have a tissue or a hankie to blow my nose. But in the concentration camp, and without a hankie, I felt I could not stand it.

"Well, why don't you pray for a hankie?" Betsie asked.

I started to laugh. There we were, with the world falling apart around us. We were locked in a camp where thousands of people were being executed each week, being beaten to death, or put through unbearable suffering—and Betsie suggests I pray for a hankie! If I were to pray for anything, it would be for something big, not something little, like that.

But before I could object, Betsie began to pray. "Father, in the name of Jesus I now pray for a hankie for Corrie, because she has a bad cold."

I shook my head and walked away. Very shortly after, I was standing by the window when I heard someone call my name. I looked out and spotted a friend of mine, another prisoner, who worked in the hospital.

"Here you are," she said in a matter-of-fact tone. "Take it. I bring you a little present."

I opened the little parcel, and inside was a handkerchief! I could hardly believe my eyes. "How did you know? Did Betsie tell you? Did you know I had a cold?"

She shrugged. "I know nothing. I was busy sewing handkerchiefs out of an old piece of sheet, and there was a voice in my heart saying, 'Take a hankie to Corrie ten Boom.' So, there is your gift. From God."

That pocket handkerchief, made from an old piece of sheet, was a message from heaven for me. It told me that there is a heavenly Father who hears, even if one of His children on this little planet prays for a tiny little thing like a hankie. Not only does He hear, but He speaks to another of His children and says, "Bring a hankie to Corrie ten Boom."

Why should I worry, when I can pray? We are God's children—His own children. Here is an old and well-known story that taught me a deep lesson.

A boy made a little ship. It was a work of art, and he had put many weeks of work into its construction. When it was ready, he took it to the river, and it could really float. He held the rope tightly in his hand, but suddenly a strong wind swept the boat away with such force that the rope broke. The river was deep and wild, and the boy knew that he had lost his ship.

After a few weeks, to his great joy, he saw his ship in the show window of a shop. He went to the shopkeeper and told him that the ship belonged to him, that he had made it. But the man said, "Only the person who gives me the price I am asking for it will have the ship."

The boy went home crying and told his father, who advised him, "I think you must try to make some money and buy the ship."

The boy worked all his spare time until he had enough money and bought his toy from the man. With his ship in his hand, he came home and said, "It's twice mine! I made it, and I bought it."

Can we trust the Lord Jesus, who made us and bought us? We surely can. We are twice His!

A minister in Russia gave me another good illustration. Many people lived in a large apartment house. All the junk was taken to the basement and it was overfull. In a corner stood a harp that was broken, and nobody was able to repair it.

Once a tramp asked if he could spend the night in the house. "There is such a severe snowstorm. May I stay here?"

"We have no room for you, but you could sleep in the basement." They emptied a corner and put some straw on the floor.

After some hours, the owner of the harp suddenly heard music in the basement. She ran downstairs and saw the tramp playing the harp.

"How did you repair my harp? I could not find anybody who was able to do it."

The tramp answered, "When I was young I made this harp, and when you make something, you can repair it."

Who made you? Do you think He can repair you?

The *No* Answer

When Betsie and I were in Ravensbruck, she became very ill. I took her to the prison hospital and she asked me, "Corrie, please pray with me. Ask the Lord Jesus to heal me. He has said, 'If you shall lay hands upon the sick they shall be healed.' Please do that for me."

I prayed and laid hands on her, and both Betsie and I trusted the Lord for healing. The next morning, I ran from the barracks and looked through the window of the hospital and found Betsie's bed was empty. I ran from window to window, until I finally saw her body. They were getting ready to take it to the crematorium. It was the darkest moment of my life.

Then, just a few days later, I was summoned to the prison office. For some reason, I was being released from prison. Surely it was a clerical error, but whatever the cause, I was free to go. It was a miracle of God.

When I came to the office, I discovered nobody there knew that Betsie was dead. So I asked, "Is my sister also free?"

"No. She stays here until the end of the war."

"Can I stay with her?"

The official became furious and shouted at me. "Disappear! Get out of here!"

Suddenly I saw God's side of what had happened. Suppose Betsie had gotten better and I had to leave her behind? I would have been forced to return to Holland and leave her alone in that horrible camp. I could not have stood it. But she had been released from the concentration camp and was now enjoying all the glory of heaven. I walked out of the camp that day praising and thanking the Lord for that un-answered prayer. Yet it really wasn't unanswered. It was answered in God's way, not mine.

So often we pray and then fret anxiously, waiting for God to hurry up and do something. All the while God is waiting for us to calm down, so He can do something through us.

There is a vast difference between prayer in faith and faith in prayer. Faith in prayer is very common. Prayer in faith is so uncommon that our Lord questions if He will find any of it on earth when He comes back. Prayer in faith is a commanded duty; it is always reverently making known our requests unto God in full confidence that, if we ask anything according to His will, He hears us; and that according to our faith an answer to our prayers will be granted us.

Praying in faith comes from an abiding faith in the Person prayed to—the confidence is in Him. It is based on a knowledge of who He is, and on a trusted conviction that He is worthy to be trusted. Praying in faith is the act of a simple-hearted child of God. Can we teach ourselves to pray in faith? We can indeed train ourselves, but the joyful experience is that it is the Spirit of God who does the job. So give room in your heart for the Holy Spirit.

From My Notebook

Prayer is opening up our sluicegates to the mighty ocean of God.

BISHOP WESTCOTT

Satan trembles when he sees
The weakest saint upon his knees.
The host of hell can that one rout,
Who meets him with a praiseful shout.

The Holy Spirit does not give a clear blueprint of the rest of your life, but only of a moment, one by one.

We can't solve problems for others. We can introduce them to the Lord.

As a camel kneels before his master to have him remove his burden at the end of the day, so kneel each night and let the Master take your burden.

If a care is too small to be turned into a prayer, it is too small to be made into a burden.

Here then is my charge: First, supplications, prayers, intercessions and thanksgivings should be made on behalf of all men. . . .

1 Timothy 2:1 PHILLIPS

Prayer is the same as the breathing of air for the lungs. Exhaling makes us get rid of our dirty air. Inhaling gives clean air. To exhale is to confess, to inhale is to be filled with the Holy Spirit.

10

Trust

You should therefore be most careful, my brothers, that there
should not be in any of you that wickedness of heart which re-
fuses to trust, and deserts the cause of the living God.

Hebrews 3:12 PHILLIPS

We continue to share in all that Christ has for us so long as
we steadily maintain, until the end, the trust with which we
began. God's love for us never changes—of this we must be
confident.

We sin, and our sin comes between our souls and God, as a
dark cloud comes between the sun and the earth, and our
communion with Him is broken. We are unable to live in the
enjoyment of God's love for us when sin stands in our way.
Our temptation to sin by worrying comes from the evil one,
but we must remember that he can only come through an
open door. Calling on Jesus' name sends him back, along with
any of his brood, because they hate and fear the name of their
Conqueror. They get away from the sound of that name as
fast as they can.

Our fearless testimony makes the power of the blood of
Jesus effective. There is great need for overcomers in this
world, and our Lord earnestly calls for men to follow in His
steps and in His strength. He won the decisive victory over

our enemies, but everyone must make that victory his own on the battlefield of his own life. In Jesus' great name, we can. By His grace, we will.

Our worry is often due to physical causes. Overwork always makes a sensitive spirit worry and hurry, which in turn overworks our nerves, until we see things in a distorted manner. It is a vicious circle, because worry usually makes us keep working harder, until we finally drop from exhaustion—physical and mental. At that point, we go to God for help, but we have already begun to listen to the devil, so we go to God with a sense of inferiority, which is the devil's message!

Some years ago, I had a very difficult problem and did not see the answer. I talked it over with a good friend. We looked at each other, and on both of our faces there was an expression of defeat. Suddenly my friend stood up. She hit the table with her hand and said, "Do we really think that the enormous power that caused Jesus to come out of the grave is not enough for our problem?" Then I saw the smallness of my faith. Yes, the same Spirit that raised Christ from the dead is willing to work in you.

But if we want to be victorious over our fears through Jesus' victory and strength, we must also be obedient. It was Jesus' obedience that defeated the enemy at every turn, until the climax of Calvary was reached.

Confessed Sins

Once we realize that fear, anxiety, and worry are sins, and then confess these sins to God, what happens? The Bible says, "He has removed our sins as far away from us as the east is from the west" (Psalms 103:12). "I've blotted out your sins; they are gone like morning mist at noon! Oh, return to me, for I have paid the price to set you free" (Isaiah 44:22). "But if we confess our sins to him, he can be depended on to forgive us and to cleanse us from every wrong . . ." (1 John 1:9).

Did you ever see a cloud again, after it had disappeared? No, the cloud that appears afterward is a different one. We do not honor God by asking forgiveness a second time for the same sin. Say, "God has beaten this thing. He had forgiven this sin and forgotten it. I can do the same in His strength." Remember that the victory has been won. Claim that victory as your own, and it will be your own in fact. There is far more victory within your reach than you have realized. Reach out your hand and take as your very own what has been done for you. Reckon yourself dead to the sin of worry.

Say with Paul, ". . . I can do everything God asks me to with the help of Christ who gives me the strength and power" (Philippians 4:13). Commit the past to God, and don't be enchained with it again.

As He cleanses our cups, He fills them to overflowing with His Holy Spirit. We must remember that our cups can be kept clean. Everything that the light of God shows as sin, we can confess and carry to the fountain of water of life, and it is gone, both from God's sight and from our hearts.

A little girl broke a beautiful antique cup. Crying, she brought it to her mother. The mother saw that the little one was sorry, and said, "I forgive you. Throw the pieces in the garbage can."

The next day, the little girl saw the pieces in the garbage can. She took them and brought them to her mother again. "I am sorry, Mother, that I broke your cup yesterday," she cried.

The mother replied, "Leave that in the garbage can, where it belongs. Remember my forgiveness." A confessed sin is dead. Give it a burial.

"Hallelujah!"

Handel's chorus was resounding through the evening air. "Hallelujah! And He shall reign for ever and ever."

I had never heard it sung so perfectly and in such beautiful surroundings.

We were in Japan. The moon and stars were as clear as they can only be in that country. Far away we even saw the white peaks of Mount Fuji.

"Hallelujah! The Lord God omnipotent reigneth."

I had never heard it sung *a capella*, without musical accompaniment. It was as if angels were singing.

I knew the girls. They were the students for whom I had been holding a daily Bible study for the last two weeks, and they were going to the same hall as I, where I was expected to answer questions.

That evening I had to listen most to their worry about sins. I prayed that the Lord would give me a clear answer for them. They were Christian girls, but what a lack of joy they had about the finished work of Jesus at the cross. I asked them a question. "When you rehearsed the 'Hallelujah Chorus,' did you make mistakes?"

The girls giggled. Japanese girls giggle much.

"Many."

"But when you were singing outside in that Japanese moonlit evening, you did not think of those mistakes, otherwise you might have repeated them. Girls, never wait to confess your sins. The devil accuses us night and day. I will tell you something. Sunday morning I spoke in your church."

"Yes, we remember it. You gave us much, but it was so short."

"I thought the same, and your pastor had promised me a long time. I asked him, 'Because I can speak only once in your church, give me as long as possible. Make your preliminaries short.' He promised me, but did not do it. We started the service at 10 o'clock, and at 11 o'clock he was still busy with the *Book of Common Prayer*. That moment the Holy Spirit showed me that I was very impatient. I knew that that was a sin, and at 11 o'clock I brought it to the Lord and asked forgiveness. When we confess our sins, He is faithful and just to forgive us and to cleanse us with His blood. Suddenly I saw that the words of the *Book of Common Prayer* were not just preliminaries, but truths that the Lord uses for His honor.

"Why did I tell you that it was 11 o'clock? Because the devil accuses us before God and our own hearts. It is possible that he said to God at 11:05, 'Do You see Corrie ten Boom in Your church and how impatient she is?' I believe that God answered him, 'I already know it. Five minutes ago Corrie told me. It is forgiven and cleansed.'

"Girls, be sure that you are always five minutes earlier than the accuser. Then you lose your worry about your sins. The reason Jesus came to earth was to save sinners. He died for you, so that you could be forgiven, and He lives for you and in you by His Holy Spirit, to make you overcomers. When you worry about your sins it is because you know them through the accuser who has told you, 'That sin is typically you. That is your nature, and you will remain like that your whole life. There is no hope for you.'

"The devil, the accuser, is a liar. When the Holy Spirit convicts you of sin, it is always in the floodlight of the finished work of Jesus at the cross. He tells you: 'Exactly for these sins Jesus died. Confess and be cleansed.'

"Do you remember what I taught you this week—what the Bible says about repented sins? 'As far as the east is from the west, so far does he remove our transgressions from us' [*see* Psalms 103]. He throws them into the depths of the sea, forgiven and forgotten, and to warn the accuser, He puts a sign saying No Fishing Allowed. Girls, instead of worrying about your sins, sing again, 'Hallelujah! King of kings and Lord of lords.' "

It sounded even more beautiful than when I had heard it outside, but this time I saw the happy faces, some still wet with tears.

The Word of God

God's promises were never meant to be thrown aside as waste paper. He intended that they should be used. God's gold is not miser's money, but is minted to be traded with. Nothing pleases our Lord better than to see His promises put into circulation; He loves to see His children bring them up to Him, and say, "Lord, do as You have said."

Charles H. Spurgeon

We deny the work of Jesus Christ and stand powerless before the enemy if we doubt the integrity of the Word of God. The bank account of the Bible is not frozen.

Someone told me, "In the Bible there are seventeen thousand promises." I don't know if that is true, but even if there were only seventeen, the quality is so great that the quantity is not too important.

. . . He has given you the whole world to use, and life and even death are your servants. He has given you all of the present and all of the future. All are yours, and you belong to Christ, and Christ is God's.

1 Corinthians 3:22, 23

When you check your inventory of blessings from God, it shows you have received good measure, pressed down and running over. Do not say, "I am too great a sinner to appropriate God's promises. Perhaps good Christians may do that, but not I." God always hears a prayer of faith. Put all your needs on the table and then say thank You.

Once a factory owner had a very expensive, complicated machine that he needed for his work. It broke down, and there was nobody who could repair it. The owner sent a telegram to the machine factory: "Send an expert." The very next day, an unimpressive man arrived at the airport. The owner sent another telegram to protest that the man they had sent was unsatisfactory. He wore old clothing, he seemed very uneducated—the owner was not at all happy with him. The answer that came back from the machine factory was, "That man is the designer of your machine."

Don't you think our own Creator can find the answers to our problems? Jesus is able to untangle all the snarls in your soul, to banish all complexes, and to transform even your fixed habit patterns. All you must do is trust Him.

From My Notebook

A dying old man said, "I am too sick to remember one promise of God. But I don't worry, because God does not forget them."

If the enemy cannot keep you from working, then he comes up behind you and pushes you and tries to kill you with overwork.

When the devil can't make you bad, he makes you busy.

Elijah was so sure of God that he added difficulties by throwing water over the altar. We, in our unbelief, try to help God.

In the forest fire, there is always one place where the fire cannot reach. It is the place where the fire has already burned itself out. Calvary is the place where the fire of God's judgment against sin burned itself out completely. It is there that we are safe.

The strength we claim from God's Word does not depend on circumstances. Circumstances will be difficult, but our strength will be sufficient.

> Your strength, my weakness—here they always meet,
> When I lay down my burden at Your feet;
> The things that seem to crush will in the end
> Be seen as rungs, on which I did ascend!

Not one sparrow (What do they cost? Two for a penny?) can fall to the ground without your Father knowing it. And the very hairs of your head are all numbered. So don't worry! You are more valuable to him than many sparrows.

Matthew 10:29–31

If you make a compromise with surrender, you can remain interested in the abundant life, all the riches of freedom, love, and peace, but it is the same as looking at a display in a shop window. You look through the window but do not go in and buy. You will not pay the price—Surrender.

E. STANLEY JONES

11

Surrender

> Jesus told him, "If you want to be perfect, go and sell everything you have and give the money to the poor, and you will have treasure in heaven; and come, follow me." But when the young man heard this, he went away sadly, for he was very rich.
>
> Matthew 19:21, 22

That rich young ruler gladly kept all the commandments, and he searched out even more ways to serve his God. But when Jesus told him he would have to give up everything he treasured in his life, the young man simply could not do it. J. H. Jowett comments on this:

> He hallowed the inch, but not the mile. He would go part of the way, but not to the end. And the peril is upon us all. We give ourselves to the Lord, but we reserve some liberties. We offer Him our home, but we mark some rooms "Private." And that word, "Private," denying the Lord admission, crucifies Him afresh.

My being a tramp for the Lord, going over the whole world, was real training for me in surrender and trust. I learned that the safest place in the world is in the center of the will of God. This is always true, even sometimes when it seems as if following God's will is physically dangerous.

Shortly after the war, I was alone in America. It was Saturday morning in Chicago. I paid the taxi driver and stepped into the YWCA. The lady in the office did not look very happy to see me.

"The office is almost closed, lady," she said.

"Have you a room for me?" I asked.

"No. Come back on Monday."

"Will you telephone the nearest police station, then, and ask them if I can sleep in a cell tonight?"

She looked very surprised. "Why?"

"Well, I come from Holland, and in Holland no woman has to stay in the street during the night. There is always room in a police station, in a cell, and I am sure that in America it will be the same. I would not think of remaining on the street all night in a town like Chicago."

She left the office for a minute, then came back and said, "We have found a room for you."

That was exactly what I had hoped would happen, and I went to my room. It was not the most beautiful room. It was very high up in the building and very small, but much more luxurious than the cell I was living in a year before, in the prison camp.

I did not go out on Sunday. It was raining, and I had discovered that when it rains in America, it pours. I needed some time for rest and for talking with the Lord. As a matter of fact, my first experience in Chicago had scared me. I did not know anyone there, and it was such a big, strange city to face alone.

That Sunday in my room, I had a good talk with the Lord. I confessed my fears to Him and surrendered the whole trip through America to His will. Two weeks after, the Lord blessed my ministry in America in a way that must have made the angels rejoice. The Lord did much good work through the many talks in all the little churches. God opened the doors and the hearts of Chicago for me, and Moody Bible

Institute gave me such a welcome that I have never since felt alone in Chicago.

My Lord knows the way through the wilderness—all I have to do is follow and to put my hand into His hand. He holds me.

There is only one force more powerful than fear, and that is faith. Does your need seem big to you? Then make sure that God knows how big it looks to your eyes, and He will treat it as such. He will never belittle it, however trivial. He will not laugh at it, or at us. He never forgets how large our problems look to us.

Does your need seem as big as the throne of grace? Do we not there—and there alone—see it in the right proportion?

We ask, "Do you believe that the Lord is your Shepherd?" "Yes, but. . . ."

That fatal word *but* shows that we do not believe the Lord is our Shepherd. "Yes, I believe it, *but* I do not have victory over my bad temper, and I am not able to win souls. I worry over things. I do not have peace and joy."

The testimony of victory puts *but* into the right place. "I am passing through a time of great sorrow and trouble, *but* the Lord is my Shepherd. I have been discouraged about my past accomplishment, *but* the Lord is my Shepherd."

Set yourself against being disturbed by disturbing things. Say to yourself, "Being upset is useless. It has bad results, it is sinful. It reproaches my Master. I will not be upset."

Amy Carmichael wrote:

He, Who loved you unto death, is speaking to you. Listen, do not be deaf and blind to Him. And as you keep quiet and listen, you will know, deep down in your heart, that you are loved. As the air is around about you, so is His love around about you now. Trust that love to guide your lives. It will never, never fail. You know how we have watched the great sea washing over the rocks, flooding them till they overflow? That is what the love of God does for us. We have no love in ourselves and our pools would soon be empty if it were not for that glorious inexhaustible sea of love which extends to you and me. Lord, do Thou turn me all into love, and all my love into obedience, and let my obedience be without interruption.

If His will be your will, and His way be your way, then all your insufficiency and inaptitude shall be met by the sufficiency of His grace.

Obey the voice of the Lord Jesus, who says, "Come unto me, all ye that labour and are heavy laden, and I will give you rest" (Matthew 11:28 KJV). Come! Like a mother says to a fearful child, "Come." Nothing else is necessary. When you come to Him, He does the job.

Jesus says, "Behold, I stand at the door, and knock: if any man hear my voice, and open the door, I will come in . . ." (Revelation 3:20 KJV).

"But as many as received him, to them gave he power to become the sons of God . . ." (John 1:12 KJV). That means to become a member of the very family of God, and ". . . Except a man be born again, he cannot see the kingdom of God" (John 3:3 KJV). We cannot expect peace or rest until we personally find it in Jesus Christ. When we do, we can say, ". . . For I know whom I have believed, and am persuaded that he is able to keep that which I have committed unto him against that day" (2 Timothy 1:12 KJV).

Know that Christ is the Lord of all: your mind, your spirit, your body. Let Christ's teachings live in your heart, making you rich in true wisdom. Put everything in His hands.

The first time a cowboy heard the story of Jesus riding on an unbroken colt, he exclaimed, "What wonderful hands He must have had!" Consider the hands of Christ: artist's hands that created all the beauty of this world; love-pierced hands of the kindest Friend that man ever had; hands that are aching to take our own and guide us in ways that are good for us; skillful hands, worthy of our trust and love.

Let us let Him clasp our hands a little tighter, and trust

Him a little more than ever before—that our paths may be straighter and gladder than in the past. Let us make more time for prayer, so that we increase the pressure of that hand on ours. Their touch is so light, and the whisper so soft, it is easy to miss them.

A young, discouraged artist fell asleep beside the picture that he was trying to complete. His master quietly entered the room, and, bending over the sleeping pupil, placed on the canvas, with his own skillful hand, the beauty that the painting lacked.

When we, tired and spent, lay down the work done in our own strength, our own great Master will make perfect our picture. He will remove every stain, every blemish, and every failure from our service. He will add the brightest luster to our service, and He will give us the highest honor for our work.

Shall we not surrender to the One who can make us His victorious artists? Paul wrote:

> My brothers, I do not consider myself to have grasped it fully even now. But I do concentrate on this: I forget all that lies behind me and with hands outstretched to whatever lies ahead I go straight for the goal—my reward the honour of my high calling by God in Christ Jesus.
>
> Philippians 3:13, 14 PHILLIPS

> Now to him who is able to keep you from falling and to present you before his glory without fault and with unspeakable joy, to the only God, our saviour, be glory and majesty, power and authority. . . .
>
> Jude 24 PHILLIPS